Building Block

by John Block

with Chris Ahrens

ISBN: 978-1-7376420-3-9

Printed in the United States of America

DEDICATION

I'M PROUD TO DEDICATE *Building Block* to my wife Margie, our daughter Allison and her husband David, our son Jeff and his wife Leanna, and their children Asher, Corban and Ezra. My family is a joyful gift from God.

Grateful thanks to Margie, without whom I wouldn't be who I am. Because of her faithfulness to God and to me and her gift of supernatural patience, she is my ultimate caregiver, helper, companion, and friend.

ACKNOWLEDGEMENTS

CO-AUTHOR: Chris Ahrens

EDITOR: John Freeman

DESIGN: Tim Brittain

COVER PAINTING: Randall M. Hasson

PATRON: Jon Sundt

To all, I offer my deep and lasting gratitude.

ON THE COVER

The luminous oil painting of John Block is the work of noted artist and calligrapher Randall M. Hasson, juxtaposed with an excerpt from "The Man in the Arena," a speech delivered by Theodore Roosevelt in Paris, France on April 23, 1910.

Original titled "Citizenship in a Republic," the speech includes this inspiring passage, which serves as an apt description of John's multi-faceted life:

"It is not the critic who counts, not the one who points out how the strong man stumbled or how the doer of deeds might have done them better...

"The credit belongs to the man who is actually in the arena, whose face is marred with sweat and dust and blood; who strives valiantly; who errs and comes short again and again;

"... who knows the great enthusiasms, the great devotions, and spends himself in a worthy cause; who, if he wins, knows the triumph of high achievement;

"... and who, if he fails, at least fails while daring greatly, so that his place shall never be with those cold and timid souls who know neither victory nor defeat."

AUTHOR'S INTRODUCTION

Lord, give me the strength

EACH DAY I PRAY THAT JESUS LIVES HIS LIFE through me with His thoughts, His words and His actions in obedience to Him.

In my life, I've done quite a few smart things, led by marrying Margie, my wife of more than 50 years.

But as she'll gladly tell you, I've done plenty of dumb things, too, with no reasonable explanation for why I did them.

Here's one of the dumbest.

In early 2002, Margie and I had just bought an off-road tent trailer, which we parked in the driveway.

I had recently recovered from surgery and we were ready to take a trip. While Margie was doing errands, I decided to hook up the trailer. I walked out the door, intending to go to our Ford Excursion and hook it up to the trailer.

Instead, I walked over to the trailer and knocked one of the two wooden blocks underneath the tires. Since the trailer was against the fence, I had to go underneath the trailer to knock the other block off.

Laying down underneath the trailer, after I knocked the block loose, I asked myself, "What have I done?"

The trailer started rolling down and would've rolled right over me if I hadn't twisted around. The axle then hit me high on my back and pinned me, forcing my chest almost to my knees.

I said, "I'm in deep trouble. There's nobody around and I know I've really hurt myself."

I was in immense pain.

Then I prayed, "Lord, you've got to help me here. Give me the strength to push this trailer back up the driveway. Or else I might die here."

So, I pushed the trailer, which I knew was at least 4,000 pounds, a few feet up the driveway so that I could lay down flat. Only after the trailer had passed completely over me as it rolled into the middle of the street was I able to stand up.

Thank you, Lord.

Every breath was painful. My entire back, from top to bottom, was in immense pain.

But, I thought, I've got to hook the trailer to the Excursion and get them out of the street. So, I did.

After that, I went into the house, laid down and then called Margie. I said, "You'd better come home. I've hurt myself and I need you to take me to the hospital, right now."

Her first response was, "You know, this is really getting old."

She called a neighbor to help me get into the car, and a few minutes later, Margie arrived to drive me to the hospital's ER.

My ER doctor, Dr. Greg Mundis, who happened to be a highly experienced back surgeon, heard my story and asked me if I was crazy.

I had broken four bones, two in my lower back and two in my upper back.

When I was in intensive care, my friend Milt Richards and my wife Margie prayed for me.

After they had left, the nurse came to me and asked if she could talk to me after her shift. It turned out that everyone in the intensive care unit had heard our prayers.

When she met with me, she told me about her marriage, and asked me to pray for her, which I did.

———∞∞∞———

Looking back on the fullness of my life, I can see God's hand in it all.

The highs and the lows, the exhilaration of victories, the disappointment and learning from defeats, and the pain that followed from pushing so hard for so long.

People always ask me if it's been worth it and my resounding answer is always "Yes!"

Why?

Because it's as Romans 11:36 (ESV) says, *"For from Him and through Him and to Him are all things. To Him be the glory forever. Amen."*

As Apostle Paul said in 1st Corinthians 15:10 ESV, *"But by the grace of God, I am what I am."*

By God's grace, this is my story.

PART 1

Early Years

CHAPTER 1

A high pain threshold

ONE OF MY EARLIEST MEMORIES is being around 3 years old and playing in our side yard.

We lived on a chicken ranch in Canoga Park, California, located on what is now Canoga Park High School. My mother was watering the front yard and I was playing with the hand-pushed rotary lawnmower leaning up against the outside wall.

I had my fingers inside the mower when suddenly it rolled away from the wall and the sharp blades rotated and cut off three of my fingers. My middle finger was hanging down, and the other two were completely cut off.

I wasn't crying or anything, but walked into the front yard, holding my hand, which was bleeding like crazy. I lifted my bloody hand and said, "Mom, look what I just did." She screamed hysterically and rushed me to the doctor, where he prepared to stitch me up.

That's when I began crying, not because of the pain, but because I was fearful of what he was going to do. Looking back, I recognize I have always had a high pain threshold.

As it turned out, I would need it.

At the medical clinic, the doctor operated on my fingers, but the middle finger was sewed on crooked. It's been bent ever since, and over the years of dunking a basketball, the finger developed a big knot, which was great for throwing a curveball when I played baseball.

My dad, John William Block, was born on September 19, 1919, in Wyoming. My mom, Zelpha Irene Adams, was born on June 11, 1916, in Benedict, Kansas. My dad was the grandson of one of three brothers who immigrated from northern Germany during the American Civil War. They first located in Missouri and became farmers.

My parents met in a "traveling car" en route traveling from Los Angeles to Kansas. A traveling car was similar to a limousine service and was used to transport groups of people to various areas in the country. In 1941, they were married.

I was born on April 16, 1944. My only other sibling, my sister Carol came along on August 10, 1945.

A hard worker who held multiple jobs when I was growing up, my dad had an enlarged heart and couldn't go in the armed services to fight in World War II. So he became a roughneck in the oil fields where he would return home each day covered with oil. He also did tractor work on various farms while my mother stayed home.

When I was 4, we moved onto a five-acre horse ranch located next to a large thoroughbred ranch. Carol and I often rode horses with our parents, in the Santa Suzanna Mountains. That's where I first fell in love with horses and the cowboy culture. I wanted to be a cowboy, like John Wayne.

Interestingly, there were similarities in our paths. He went to Glendale High, so did I. He was inducted into the Glendale High School Athletic Hall of Fame, so was I. He went to USC and was in the Sigma Chi fraternity, and so did I. He would come to have faith in God, and so did I.

When I was about 5 years old, while on the ranch, I was moving an irrigation-spiked sprinkler. I dropped it on my right foot, piercing it. My mom again took me to the medical clinic.

After that, I was playing on a wooden railing on one of the stalls. I had shorts on, and as I slid along the railing, I put a huge splinter into my upper inside thigh. She again took me to the medical clinic.

I still have the scar.

Another day, I must have been mad at my parents because I said, "I'm leaving home."

"Go ahead," said my dad.

I stormed out of the house and got about halfway across a pasture and turned around, realizing I had nowhere to go being only 5 years old.

CHAPTER 2

'He is a bad boy'

WE MOVED TO GLENDALE where my first-grade teacher gave me one of the greatest gifts ever in teaching me to read phonetically.

Once I knew how to read, I went to the library and read everything I could find about various American heroes, especially baseball heroes.

Baseball was my passion, and when I wasn't playing it, I was reading all about the game and its players. One of the books was about Lou Gehrig, who was so determined to hang onto his position that he played through any and all injuries, including broken bones.

I wanted to be like Lou Gehrig.

When I entered 2nd grade, I had a very embarrassing experience. After the girl sitting in the desk in front of me dropped her really cool pencil, I picked it up and hid it from her. She reported it to the teacher, who asked who had taken her pencil.

I remained silent, scared to death until the teacher searched me, found the pencil, and then declared to the class, "Don't trust John Block, he is a bad boy!"

I've never forgotten that.

About that time, I was home alone and playing with matches burning toilet paper, when I lit our wooden toilet seat on fire. When my dad got home, he said, "I'm going to get the owner of the house so you can apologize to him."

After the owner arrived, I said I was sorry. Then, my dad took me behind the couch and whipped me with his belt. I never played with fire again.

My dad got me a bicycle that I loved riding. When I came home from school one day, my sister was riding it on the street near our house. I told her to get off and she wouldn't.

Not long after that, she was riding fast when I grabbed the handlebars and she went flying, landing on her head, shearing off her front teeth. My dad and mother drove her to the medical clinic with me and told me to stay in the car. I don't recall her crying much, and I learned over time that she was a very tough little girl.

After a while, my dad came and sat with me in the car, telling me to pray for my sister, which I did.

That's the first time I remember praying.

When I started Little League baseball, my dad practiced with me for several hours each day. He helped me work on my batting, fielding, and pitching skills. He was also a coach of the Fire Department Little League team. I was good enough to make the all-star team every year.

I was pitching the final inning of a game, and all I had to do was get the other team out for the win. Instead, I loaded the bases and walked a player in for their win. I walked off the field, crying when my dad came onto the field, put his arm around me and walked me back to the car without saying a word.

That was the best thing he could have done.

I started Cotillion and learned dance steps and figures, combining them with proper etiquette to form a social education program. The boys wore suits, and the girls wore nice Sunday dresses. At first, it scared me to death.

We learned dance steps such as the jitterbug, two-step, waltz, cha-cha, foxtrot, and the minuet. We were taught to make eye contact while speaking to adults, to introduce ourselves with a firm handshake, and to display common courtesy, manners, kindness, and respect.

Dancing provided an athletic foundation for my life. It helped me both as a young man and as an athlete, since basketball and baseball require grace of movement with rhythm and good footwork.

Nearly every day after school I walked to the YMCA where I learned swimming, ping-pong, and music. A guy played guitar and we sang along to songs like O Suzanna and other old country folk songs.

We attended the Methodist Church, and I became part of the youth choir. When Disneyland opened in 1955, they brought our choir in at Christmas time. I attended for free, and wow, did I love that. I was in the church choir and school glee club through junior high.

Along with prayer and Bible study, music has always been a big part of my life.

CHAPTER 3

The value of working hard

WHEN I WAS 11, my dad bought a gas station in the city of Montrose near the foothills of the Angeles National Forest. After school, I would walk, bike or hitchhike the five miles to the station every day to begin work with my dad.

It was a full-service gas station where an attendant pumped gas, cleaned windows, checked tires, and the radiator. My dad taught me how to change oil, repair tires, do sparkplugs, tune-ups, lubes, and keep the station clean. He taught me to drive the cars onto the lube rack and to wash and clean them.

Whenever I had a spare moment, I cleaned the gas pump, the islands, and all the floors. He worked hard and I learned the value of working hard. Within a couple years he realized I was able to work the station alone.

It was over 100 degrees when an older model Cadillac pulled into the station with a steaming radiator. The driver turned off the engine and asked me to check the radiator. I lifted the hood and removed the radiator cap.

When I loosened the cap the pressure of the radiator blew boiling water everywhere. In response, I jerked my head back and I hit it on the hood.

When I ducked back down, the water came down on the back of my neck and shoulders.

Guess what else I never did again?

When I yelled, my dad came running, He took me inside the station and got some strong hand cleaner and rubbed it over my neck and shoulders. I was severely burned, and he rushed me to the doctor's office.

The doctor said I had third-degree burns, but it would have been a lot worse if my dad hadn't put that cleanser on me. His actions prevented an infection. I spent hours that night pacing and circling the kitchen table in pain.

Not long afterward, I fixed a spare tire on another old Caddy. It had a trunk that automatically screwed down. I put the tire back in the trunk and closed it. It screwed down on all my fingers.

I yelled, "Hey, Dad, can you come out here and pop the trunk? I think I've hurt my fingers."

I lost the nails on every finger except my thumbs.

I always loved bicycles and bought this old beat-up Schwinn and fixed it up with new parts. My dad taught me how to sand the frame down to the metal, so it looked like chrome. I then sealed the frame with clear lacquer, and I think I had the only chrome bike in Glendale.

When I was 15, Dad bought a beat-up two-door 1949 Ford coupe. Even though I wasn't old enough to legally drive, he gave it to me to fix up so I could drive it when I turned 16. We fixed the engine and installed new dual exhausts.

Later, we drove to Tijuana to have the entire interior re-upholstered. I sanded the whole car, put primer on, and drove it to Earl Scheib, where $29.99 bought a beautiful black paint job. It was a sweet car.

I had that car through high school and on weekends I'd cruise the town and Bob's Big Boy with some of my teammates.

PART 2

High school

CHAPTER 1

'You're not playing baseball'

WHEN I WAS A SOPHOMORE at Glendale High School, baseball was my first love. Our school had a tremendous baseball program and we had been CIF (California Interscholastic Federation) champions the previous year.

A pivotal moment in my life came when the assistant basketball coach, Ed Goorjian, physically pulled me out of the line where I was about to sign up for year-around baseball. He said, "Block, you're not playing baseball. You're playing basketball."

I said, "Okay, but I've got to talk to my parents first." My dad said that was fine.

One of the team stipulations, however, was that I had to have a buzz haircut, like everyone else on the team.

After my dad took me to the barber and they cut off my long, wavy hair, he said, "Now listen. Your mom is going to be really upset about this. Don't say anything. I'll handle it."

When we walked into the house, my mom saw my haircut, and started crying. I made some smart aleck remark and my dad immediately turned around and slugged me in the stomach.

He wanted me to realize I had disobeyed him, and I never made a smart aleck remark to my mom again. I loved my dad and I knew that I had disobeyed him. I believed I deserved what I got.

I was 15 years old, 6-2 and 150 pounds when I went out for the basketball team. I was skinny, but very athletic. We had some great players, like Tom Dose, who was all-CIF and later played for Stanford. They put me on varsity although I was only in 10th grade and had never seriously played basketball before.

My life changed when I grew six inches during the basketball season. I grew two inches in two weeks and was in bed aching, feverish and just growing. My parents were panicked, and when I finally got out of bed, my pants were two inches shorter than before.

As a result of such quick growth, I lost most of my coordination and was very awkward.

When the season ended, I went out for baseball. I was now 6-8, 155 pounds. On the first day of baseball practice, I was in my practice uniform when Coach Gelsinger, a biology teacher, walked up to me, slapped his hand against his head and said, "My God, Block, I believe you could tread water in a test tube!"

I played different positions — pitcher, first base and outfield. I was a hard thrower, but still uncoordinated, so I couldn't control the direction of the pitches. I beaned a teammate in practice once, and that was the end of my career as a pitcher.

After the school year was over, head basketball coach Gene Haas and his assistant Dick Davis gave me a basket with a wooden backboard to set up on my garage. They also gave me a squat rack with weights and a jump rope.

I was very dedicated to working out and had the squat rack and weights in my bedroom. Soon, I got to the point where I could quarter-squat 500 pounds.

The jump rope became a huge part of my training, and I continued jumping rope all the way through my NBA career. I still recommend jumping rope to help young players build athleticism. It helps with rhythm, concentration, balance, quickness, speed and competitiveness.

You count your jumps and are always pushing yourself to be better and better, making fewer mistakes.

By working with the weights and the jump rope, my vertical jump improved six inches in one summer.

That summer, Dick Davis, a UCLA graduate and a very high-level beach volleyball player, became the varsity head coach. He had a beach volleyball camp in Huntington Beach that I attended because Coach Davis said it would help build my athletic ability.

It was a great opportunity to learn beach volleyball, which I played until my 50s when I had to quit because I had just had my ankle fused and was developing severe neuropathy.

CHAPTER 2

We built a strong friendship

By my junior year, my dad sold the gas station in Montrose and bought another newly built gas station in Chevy Chase Canyon, an upscale neighborhood.

The gas station was the only business in the area that bordered the Chevy Chase Country Club, where Coach Davis was a member and frequently played.

During the offseason, I was able to take some time off from the gas station to have him teach me to play golf.

During basketball season of my junior year, one of my teammates, Dick Weaver, a senior who ended up playing basketball at Stanford, invited me to a Young Life club. Young Life is an organization reaching out to high school kids to present the Gospel of Jesus Christ through the building of personal relationships.

Bob Reverts, the Young Life leader who led the club, had played basketball at Tennessee. After I met him, he began attending my practices. After practice, he would work with me on my fundamentals and moves. It impressed me that he would take the time to help me with my game.

We built a strong friendship that extended beyond the basketball court and club meetings.

Toward the end of the school year, Bob suggested I attend a Young Life camp called Frontier Ranch in Buena Vista, Colorado. He arranged a scholarship for me. As anyone who's ever been to a Young Life camp will tell you, it's one of the best weeks of their life. It certainly was for me.

Throughout the week, a speaker systematically laid out the gospel of Jesus through stories and His words from the Scriptures.

Even though I had grown up in the Methodist Church, this was the first time I heard the Gospel of Jesus Christ explained in a meaningful way.

After one of the last meetings, our cabin leader Terry Olsen took me to a point overlooking the mountains. He asked if I wanted to accept Jesus as my Lord and Savior. I'll never forget my response.

I said, "Well, I guess so," and we prayed together.

The next morning when I awoke, I knew something had changed in my life. I didn't know what it all meant, but something had happened to me.

I now realize that Jesus had entered my life and I became a totally new person.

I drove my 1949 Ford to school every day. One day during my senior year, I came out to get my car and found it missing. It turns out my sister had taken it. She had taken my key and made a copy for herself. Oh, I was not happy. To avoid that happening again, I removed the distributor wire so she couldn't start the car.

A few days later, after practice I came out and my car was gone again. She figured out what I had done, got another distributor wire from another car, installed it and took my car. She and I were always kind of battling.

It wasn't until years later that she began sharing how I always got the attention from my parents and was in the newspapers. I was always with my dad, and I was always the "star."

She believed that she didn't get the same kind of affection, attention, or affirmation that I did. My dad loved my sister, but had a hard time expressing it.

Sadly, sports for young girls were not really available in school at that time. My sister could have been a good athlete and she was certainly competitive.

CHAPTER 3

In many ways supernatural

TOWARD THE END OF MY SENIOR YEAR, we had lost only two games and were undefeated in league play. The next week, we were headed for the CIF playoffs. We won our last league game against our crosstown rival, Glendale-Hoover High.

It was Saturday night, and I went out after the game with a girlfriend, who was a cheerleader. I got home around 1 am, surprised that my dad was still awake. I said, "Dad, why are you still up?" He said, "I didn't have a very good night. I had to stand during the game because I wasn't feeling well."

We talked a bit, and I went to bed.

About two hours later, my mother came into my room, hysterically telling me, "Your dad's had a heart attack. Go in and see what you can do. I'll call 911."

I went into his room and tried to resuscitate him using mouth-to-mouth and everything I knew to do. But he had died of a massive heart attack at the age of 42.

I was 17.

As I look back, something happened that was in many ways supernatural. I didn't really know how to pray, and I never asked the question why my dad had died. Instead, from that moment on, in difficult times I asked God, "What are you trying to teach me through this?"

When the ambulance was on its way, I went out on our front porch and prayed, "Lord, I'm not sure what just happened, but you're going to have to give me the strength and the ability to help my mother and my sister through this."

I realized many years later that God had given me a strong measure of faith.

He answered my prayer and gave me what I needed to help my mother and sister get through that challenging time.

My dad had died around 3 am, Sunday morning, and my coach, Dick Davis, came over later that day to be with me, which was really meaningful. The first round of the CIF playoffs was beginning that Tuesday.

I was probably numb from the loss of my father, but when I returned to school on Monday, neither my classmates nor my teammates said anything about his passing, which I actually appreciated. The next evening, when we played our first playoff game, I did my best to keep focused on basketball.

My mother and I knew that my dad would want me to play.

CHAPTER 4

Crying in the locker room

WE GOT TO THE CIF semifinals against Chaffey High, a scrappy and well-coached team.

The Cal State Los Angeles gym was packed, so it was somewhat difficult for me to see my mother, grandfather and his wife, and my sister, even though they were sitting in the stands right behind our bench.

They were all highly emotional, but I tried not to let their emotions affect me.

The game was tight, and we were down by one point with around 15 seconds left. The coach called a play to set me up for an easy shot. It worked perfectly, but I missed the shot, got the rebound, missed again, got the rebound, shot again and got fouled.

With seconds left in the game, I had two free throws, one to tie, the next one to win. I missed both and we lost the game.

I was crying in the locker room from a combination of losing the game and grief. Coach Davis came up, laid a hand on me and said it was okay. I knew what he meant, and it was comforting. It was similar to that time years earlier when my dad comforted me after losing a baseball game.

I was being recruited by USC, along with Bill Westphal, who became one of my lifelong best friends. We had played against each other in the Pacific Shores Basketball Tournament.

He came from a Christian family and USC thought it would be good to put the two of us together in the recruiting process, which included eating meals and going to USC football games in the Los Angeles Coliseum.

After we were both offered full basketball scholarships, we decided to commit to USC. That meant we'd join Gary Sutherland, one of my high school teammates on the basketball and baseball teams, and who had committed to USC on a baseball scholarship.

My early decision to go to USC was God-directed. I can't imagine what it would've been like if I had to go through the recruiting process without my dad, and the pressure that would have put on my mother.

Soon after my dad died, Bill asked me to come to his house and hang out with the family. There were two girls in the family. One was Bill's twin sister, Carol, the other was Laurel, and the youngest family member was Paul, who was 10 at the time.

I ended up going there almost every weekend, and played highly competitive two-on-two games in their driveway with Bill, Paul and their dad.

Bill was to become one of the most successful basketball coaches that I've ever known. Paul would become a Hall of Fame basketball player and a successful college and NBA basketball coach, and one of my closest, dearest friends. I reflect on his life as I am writing this book.

He died of brain cancer on January 2, 2021.

Paul and I remained close friends until he went to be with the Lord. Our faith in Jesus was the foundation of this friendship. Over the years we competed in many different sports with and against each other. We were there for each other and our families in the good times and the bad times.

Paul was always full of surprises. Like the time I was at a conference in Phoenix and he asked me to have dinner with him and his wife, Cindy, at their favorite Mexican food restaurant. He said he had a surprise for me.

When he picked me up at the hotel, in the front seat, sitting with Paul was Rush Limbaugh. That was some surprise!

Over two years had passed since my dad's death. My mom had to sell the two gas stations and our house. I came home to her apartment one weekend, and she was depressed and crying. I said, "Mom, it's time for you to stop your mourning and get on with life. Take a look at your daughter. She really needs you."

As soon as I said those words, she snapped right out of it.

She knew it was true, and she stopped mourning.

She had gone to work for Forest Lawn Cemetery where my dad was buried. She worked there for years, and I think that was part of how she coped. She was in administration, and she helped people dealing with the loss of loved ones.

Looking back, I was never very close to my mother. It was rare that I was able to talk with her or do things with her, and I think she wanted it that way. She was highly independent, and seemed closer to my sister. When my sister was facing challenges, my mother was there to help.

Meanwhile, during the spring of my senior year in high school, I was a member of both the baseball and track teams.

As a naturally fast runner, I ran a 50-flat 440, which is 440 yards, pretty fast for a 6-8 high school basketball player. By comparison, when Wilt Chamberlain was in high school, he ran the 440 in 48 seconds.

I ended up competing in the high jump in some high school track meets as I could jump over six feet, even though I had no form.

One time, right after I played a baseball game, I hopped a fence and high-jumped in a track meet. No problem.

PART 3

Glendale College

CHAPTER 1

Thousands of shots

AFTER I GRADUATED from Glendale High, I had hoped to go to USC.

Problem was, my grades weren't good enough because I lacked a couple of required courses. So, I decided to enroll in Glendale Community College to take the necessary classes, bring up my GPA, and then join Bill and Gary at USC.

At first, I wasn't planning on playing basketball at Glendale. My plan was to go there for one semester and transfer to USC, which is what I did.

Abe Androff, the head coach at Glendale College, convinced the coaches at USC that it would be better if I played 21 games at Glendale rather than the 16 freshman games at USC. That way, he'd be able to coach me individually.

Coach Androff had been the captain of the basketball team at USC back in 1948. He was a tremendous coach and teacher. From the time I began attending classes at Glendale, he spent hours and hours teaching me and drilling me how to shoot and play the post position.

He would rebound for me as I took thousands of shots before official practice began. He taught me footwork, body positioning, and movement.

He told me the great free throwers are not bothered by distraction. He said, "You hold and set the ball so all you can see is the rim. You want to get it just over the front of the rim. This teaches you how to get the right arc with touch."

He taught me to stand right in front of the rim and swish the shot, not hitting the rim.

I had to make 100 shots in a row before he would move me one step back. Then, I would take a step back, and I'd make another 100 in a row.

When I finally got to the free-throw line, I kept track of my makes and misses, counting in tens, shooting hundreds of free throws every day.

I didn't spend much time with Coach Androff, except on the court, but the foundation of his teaching remains with me to this day.

He taught me to break things down in the simplest way and work on it until the moves become more complex. He taught me offensive post moves and developed an offense that revolved around me.

Coach Androff had us running up hills to help condition us. There was a tradition that every year the basketball team would race the cross-county track team. The race was held at Verdugo Park, a huge park near the college.

The course was about three miles, and the basketball team was given about a half-mile head start.

The cross-country team had won the State Championships the last two years, and they had never been beaten by the basketball team.

Of course, that fired me up and I thought, *We're gonna beat 'em.*

Don Sigaty, who was Glendale College's basketball MVP that season, came in first, and I came in second. For the first time ever, the basketball team beat the cross-country team, and it wasn't even close.

I had averaged 17 points a game in high school, but I learned so much from Coach Androff that I was soon averaging 26.3. The one game that stands out that season was at Trade Tech College. I fouled out three guys and scored 58 points, which was a school record. I also shot 18-for-24 from the free-throw line.

We were 7–0 in the league when I left Glendale to go to USC. While at Glendale, I was the second-leading scorer in the league even though the leading scorer played seven more games than I did. If I had stayed there, we might have been able to win a State Championship for Coach Androff.

When I transferred to USC in the second semester of 1963, I roomed with Gary Sutherland in Marks Hall, an athletic dorm. I began as a business major, and after one semester transferred to a physical education major.

That summer USC got me a job, the worst job possible for me, even though it paid good money.

I was placed on an assembly line for the Arden Ice Cream company, stacking and wrapping boxes of ice cream bars with a string machine. The machine was tricky, and I had to concentrate on my work because it was unbelievably boring.

The only good part of the job was that I got to wrap boxes of Heath Bars — which soon became my all-time favorite ice cream bar.

Once in a while, the workers who placed the bars in the box would miss one. It came down the conveyor belt, and was just thrown away. It was so lonely I thought it just needed to be eaten. Scoring points in basketball may not have been my only record — I once ate 32 ice cream bars in one day!

Because of my irresistible love of Heath Bars, and messing up the machine, I was fired after three weeks.

CHAPTER 2

The shot fell short of the rim

BY MY SOPHOMORE YEAR, I was 6-9, but only weighed 185 pounds. I was strong, but not strong enough to go against some of the strongest players in NCAA D-1.

One of those players was George Unseld, brother of Wes Unseld, who is in the Naismith Memorial Basketball Hall of Fame. On my first road trip with USC, we traveled with UCLA, the NCAA Champions that year and our highly-charged crosstown rival.

We were playing a double-header — we played Kansas, the host team, and UCLA played Kansas State.

What scheduling — Wooden won again, in the scheduling war.

Unseld was the center for Kansas, and one of my first moves against him was a sweeping, moving, right-hand hook shot that I had learned at Glendale College. I dribbled across the key about ten feet from the rim and attempted a hook shot.

The shot fell short of the rim because Unseld had moved me out to the free-throw line. I never shot a running hook shot again.

Okay, maybe once more.

In the NBA, I once tried shooting it against the legendary Kareem Abdul-Jabbar when he was with the Milwaukee Bucks. But he anticipated what I was planning, and he didn't just block the shot, he caught the ball out of the air. We lost our game against Kansas, and UCLA won against Kansas State.

Keith Erickson, who played for UCLA, was a friend of my teammate, Ron Wey. Keith earned headlines by shutting down Kansas State All-American Willie Murrell.

When we had our team meeting to talk about strategy for the Kansas State game, Coach Forest Twogood asked, "Who's going to guard Willie Murrell?"

Ron said, "I will."

Coach Twogood, who hated UCLA, said, "Ron, that's because your buddy, Keith Erickson, shut him down."

Ron did guard him, but Murrell had a very good game and we lost again. One play that will always stand out in my memory was when Murrell was driving down the middle of the court. Ron was just over the half-court line backpedaling as Murrell came right at him.

As was his habit, Ron hitched his shorts up, wiped sweat from his nose, and just as he did, Murrell blew by Ron and scored with a thundering dunk.

The play didn't seem all that memorable until Monday after the trip when Coach Twogood played the game film for us on a 16mm projector with a rewind button. When it came to the play where Murrell blew by Ron and dunked, we saw Ron hitching up his pants and wiping sweat from his nose.

Coach Twogood must have run that back and forth ten or more times, saying, "Ronnie, you're picking your nose as Murrell is blowing past you." We were embarrassed for Ron. He got up and walked out of the session. The next day he quit the team, a decision he regrets to this day.

That road trip to Kansas was a real eye-opener for me, playing in my first D-1 games. In community college I was scoring a lot and now I was only averaging around 13 points a game. I quickly learned that going from high school to junior college wasn't such a huge leap, but going to D-1 college basketball was.

Next, we played an away game against Arizona State, who had a tremendous player in Joe Caldwell, who went on to play six seasons in the NBA and five in the ABA.

During the game, Joe was coming down the middle of court and I was the only player back on defense. I was setting up for a charge in the middle of the key when he jumped over me and dunked the ball.

I was what they would now call "posterized."

Another tough player was the center for UCLA, Fred Slaughter. Fred was 260 pounds and extremely fast. I was fast, too, and the first time we played, I stayed with him wherever he went. I told him, "Fred, you're not going anywhere without me being right with you."

He grabbed the front of my jersey, pulled me to him and said, "Don't you ever talk to me again." I didn't. That year I was both frustrated and intense, so much so that of the 14 games we played in the Pac-8, I led the league with 60 fouls.

During that sophomore year, Gary Sutherland and I joined the Sigma Chi fraternity. My "big brother" in the fraternity was Bob Selleck, who was a very good baseball pitcher and younger brother of Tom Selleck, the now-famous actor who was my teammate during my senior year at USC.

The fraternity was like "Animal House," and the fraternity later got kicked off campus.

I was a loner and a new believer in Jesus, although I had little idea what that really meant.

CHAPTER 3

'I'd love to, but I can't afford it'

I DECIDED THAT FRATERNITY LIFE wasn't for me and by the end of the semester, I was nearly flunking out. Coach Twogood told Gary and me to get out of Sigma Chi and move into a dorm or else we'd lose our scholarships.

So, we moved into an older dorm that was built in the 1920s as a hotel and was now called Touton Hall, which everyone called "Rootin Tootin Hall."

During semester break our grades came out and confirmed the worst, that we weren't going to be academically eligible to play. The coaches requested that Gary and I talk to the professor and try to arrange to take the final again.

We had two days before we flew to Cal Berkeley to play in our first Pac-8 game. We studied all night to pass the test. We took the test and left on our trip not knowing if we had passed or not. The next day at the pre-game meal a guy walked up in front of the entire team and spoke to Coach Twogood.

Coach said, "Sutherland, Block — you both passed and are eligible!" We were obviously extremely relieved. Then Coach told us, "You'd better have a heck of a game."

I was frustrated and angry because I had a poor season. Since basketball was the center of my life at the time, I thought that everything was falling apart. Bill Westphal sensed this and suggested that I go to Hollywood Presbyterian Church with him to meet the college department's pastor, Don Williams.

Don was fresh out of Princeton and Union Seminary, where he had earned his PhD on the Epistles of Paul. I was 19 at the time and Don was in his mid-20s. He had taken over this huge college department that had been started and led by Henrietta Mears, who later made a significant impact on modern evangelical Christianity.

Early on, she had started a faith-based camp called Forest Home in the San Bernardino Mountains.

I went to a Sunday morning college department meeting with Bill, where Don was teaching from the Scriptures. I was amazed to see over 300 students there. Afterward, I met Don and discovered we had both been in Young Life at Glendale High.

He said, "I'm speaking at a Young Life camp at Forest Home next weekend. Would you like to come along?" I said, "I'd love to, but I can't afford it."

He said, "Don't worry about that. You will stay with me."

The next weekend I went to Forest Home, and after Don spoke, we sat down at the snack bar, and he asked me about my dad. I told him about the night he died, and for the first time in two years I mourned my dad, and just let it all out.

That forged the beginning of one of the strongest relationships I've had in my life.

Don asked if I would be interested in us meeting together regularly, so I could learn how to study the Bible and how to pray. He taught me how to study the Bible inductively.

We met regularly in my dorm room where he continued teaching me about the Scriptures and prayer.

Prior to that, I had rarely prayed, and never out loud. Don said, "Let's have a conversation with God where I pray a sentence and you pray a sentence. We'll just talk to God, thank Him, and make requests."

I'd been unbelievably shy, but that process of prayer began to slowly break down that shyness.

After one of those times together in my dorm room, I walked Don out to his car, leaned down to the window and thanked him, saying, "I hope one day I'll do what you're doing."

That turned out to be prophetic for the two of us, as the Lord put us together in a way that changed both our lives. For the rest of my life, God called me into teaching and discipling others.

While things had improved, I remained frustrated with myself and one day I told Don, "I have got to get my emotions and anger under control." I had been swearing all the time, something that still pops up occasionally. It's an ongoing battle.

Don said, "Anytime you catch yourself swearing or getting angry, just pray, 'Lord, forgive me and help me to conquer this.' It doesn't matter when it occurs, when you recognize it's happening or has happened, go to God."

It didn't take long until I was going directly to God, and I soon began gaining control over my frustration and anger.

Now I'll say, "Lord, forgive me for that coming out of my mouth. I just lost it for a minute." The advice from Don changed the way I approached basketball and life. Because of his mentoring, I can now pass that message on.

During the summer after my sophomore year, USC arranged a job for me with a rendering company, picking up barrels of bones and fat from butcher shops. We worked four days a week, two of them up to 12 hours a day, and had Wednesday off.

They put me on a route that included Glendale, La Crescenta and parts of the San Fernando Valley, my home area.

My job was to roll these 300-pound drums, sometimes for long distances, and put them into a bucket that was lifted up into the truck. The work built up my forearms and wrists and I became much stronger.

I loved that job.

CHAPTER 4

'I can get you some stuff'

DURING MY JUNIOR YEAR, Bill Westphal, Doug Bolcom and I moved into an apartment with Don Williams, where we started a Bible study for athletes.

Future tennis legend Stan Smith was part of the original group, along with Lew Hoyt, who had won the NCAA championships in high jump after clearing seven feet.

I was still only 185 pounds and needed to gain weight to be more competitive on the court. A good friend of mine whose dad was a pharmacist said, "I can get you some stuff to help you gain weight."

He meant steroids, but I had no idea what those were at the time. I only cared that it worked. He got me a steroid called Dianabol. I took it for three weeks and gained 20 pounds. It worked, but the side effects were horrendous.

After the three weeks were over, the physical side effects ended but the emotional effects continued. In practices and games, I could not control my emotions. I was angry and on edge all the time. It got so bad during the season that our trainer gave me downers just to get me through the games.

It wasn't until halfway through the season that the emotional side effects from steroids ended.

I was now 205 pounds, the weight I would maintain for the next six years. Even without steroids, however, I was a very intense individual who hated losing because I hated not measuring up to what I knew I was capable of.

That year we had a winning season where our team's forward Allen Young and I both averaged 16 points. I averaged 9 rebounds that year and he averaged 10. I had played against him in high school when he was at Glendale-Hoover High, our crosstown rival.

During Easter break of my junior year at USC, I "worked" maintenance at the school track, cleaning the track area. I was in boots, jeans and a T-shirt when Lew Hoyt, who was practicing the high jump, asked me if I had ever high-jumped. I told him I had cleared six feet in high school.

He set the bar to five-something and eventually I went over six feet wearing boots.

He told me that his two backup high-jumpers were hurt and that he would ask the coach if I could compete for the team. In my first dual track meet in the Los Angeles Coliseum, I jumped over six feet, two inches and took third.

The next weekend, also in the Coliseum, the meet was against UCLA and I took another third. In the yearbook that year, I'm in the team picture with the track team. The jumpers whose place I had taken recovered, or I could've placed in one more event and lettered in track.

That would've been cool.

PART 4

Meeting Margie

CHAPTER 1

'Who's that girl?'

DURING THAT TIME, Don Williams put together a work-study retreat at Forest Home. There were 13 or 14 gals and as many guys at the retreat. I was sitting in the Roundhouse snack bar with a young married couple, Steve and Margie Haas, who were adult sponsors.

Steve was a tremendous athlete who had held the U.S. record for the 100-yard dash, 220, 440 and 880. Just before dinner, a gal taking a shortcut walked through the door on her way to the dining room. I still remember what she was wearing—a mustard colored parka, brown knickers, and after-ski boots.

She had blond hair, and as soon as she walked in, I nudged Steve and said, "That's the girl I'm going to marry."

Over the years I've talked to a lot of guys about the right girl. Now I realize that only God knows who that is. In scriptures, God always brings the woman to the man. From that moment on, I knew 100 per cent that God alone had brought Margie to me.

Don Williams, who was running the conference, was about to pray over dinner when I walked up to him and asked, "Who's that girl?"

He told me her name was Margie Papke, and I said, "Could you put me on work detail with her tomorrow?" He did, and we worked together the entire next day cleaning and painting cabins.

Our first date was at dinner at the Haas' home for my 21st birthday. She was 17. Bill Westphal was also there with his date. I had borrowed my brother-in-law's amazing Jaguar convertible to impress Margie. We had a great time.

She was living in the woman's dorm at USC and I was on a meal plan that used the same cafeteria as her dorm. We ended up eating many meals together for the rest of the semester.

One day we were walking across campus together when we sat down on a bench to talk. We had only been dating for about a month or so when I told her, "We're going to get married."

She looked at me and said, "Are you crazy? I'm 18, and I have to graduate from college. After that I'm going to be traveling in Europe, and then I have a year of internship." She was studying to be an occupational therapist.

I said, "That's no problem, I'll be waiting for you whenever you're ready, because we're gonna get married. I don't care how long it takes."

I had no money, so our first dates were often in the recreation room where we played ping-pong. Since Margie was just learning the game, I played sitting down and with my left hand. Even now when we play ping-pong, we remember those times and laugh.

PART 5

A Harlem summer

CHAPTER 1

The only white guy on the court

EVERY SUMMER, Hollywood Presbyterian Church's college department would send out short-term mission teams.

They often traveled out of the country, but that year it was to New York City. Going on that trip wasn't even on my mind because I had to work that summer in order to have enough money for the following year.

One Saturday night, instead of staying at my apartment at USC, I drove home and stayed overnight with my mother in Glendale. I had gone to bed fairly late, and around midnight God spoke to my spirit, saying, "You're going to Harlem, New York."

Knowing that God had spoken, I immediately got up and called Don Williams right then. I said, "I believe God just told me. I'm going to Harlem, New York."

He replied, "That's amazing. Tomorrow we're selecting the people to go to Harlem. You'll be going."

That June there were about 15 of us on a train, going from Los Angeles to New York City. It took four days with an overnight stop in Chicago. I slept on the floor because there were no comfortable seats for a six-nine basketball player.

Bill Westphal was with us and was assigned to go to the Lower Eastside while I was assigned to Harlem.

Once in Harlem, the entire group gathered at a small black church called Church of the Master, on Morningside Drive, just below Columbia University. We had our orientation there along with what was probably the most significant and emotional communion of my life, administered by the black pastor of the church.

My task was to build relationships through playing basketball on the courts of Harlem.

Young Life put me into an apartment with four or five local players. My roommates kept varying. Some of them, like Bob Spivey, were really good guys. Spivey and I hit it off, and he knew all the top playgrounds where big-time basketball was played by some of Harlem's legends.

We would go to these playgrounds all around town and I would be the only white guy on the court.

The courts were usually asphalt with a chain link fence around it, placed only a couple of feet from the backboard. The pole was straight up and down with a metal backboard and no net.

I loved driving to the basket but my opponents were always pounding me, knocking me into the pole or the fence. Fouls were not called and if you called one, you'd better be ready to fight. On these courts, when you lost you had to wait your turn to play again, sometimes for hours.

That wasn't going to happen to me, and I very rarely left the court.

Very quickly, I learned to be even more aggressive and tougher than I had been, to initiate contact and still be able to score. Without that summer in Harlem, there's no possible way I'd develop into the player I became.

CHAPTER 2

A nocturnal creature

AFTER GAMES, I started going into the Projects to visit with some of my teammates who lived there.

For the first time in my life, I was exposed to extreme poverty where three families often shared one apartment. Families would do three shifts — one family living there for eight hours before another came in.

When you walked the streets of Harlem, you would see children playing on the street at 3 in the morning because they had no home to go to.

Summer was especially difficult for me in the inner-city. Starting off, there were four of us in our one-bedroom apartment. We all slept on mattresses on the floor, and at times there were up to 12 of us crammed into that little space.

I soon became a nocturnal creature, and rarely went to bed before 2 or 3 in the morning, which was the culture of the Projects.

Without air conditioning, it was really hot most of the time. One escape was the theater where we sometimes went at 9 in the morning after buying a movie ticket for ten cents. It didn't matter much what the movie was, we just wanted to sit in the air-conditioning.

It was 1965, the summer after the Harlem Riots. A group of us were at Coney Island when we heard that the Watts Riots were taking place. My Harlem friends knew I was from LA, and they said, "John, you're way safer here than you would be in LA."

I said, "Yeah, I believe I am."

They used to have what were called "Latin Concerts" in the Harlem region of Central Park. I loved music and dancing, and I asked my friends if I could go with them. "No way, it's far too dangerous, and you wouldn't last five minutes," they told me.

One day Bob Spivey and two or three others of us were walking from a court back to our apartment when we stopped at a stoplight. I was the only white guy on the street.

As we were waiting to cross, this guy standing near me asked, "Man, how tall are you?" "I'm 6-9," I said.

He then pulled out this huge switchblade, and serious as he could be, told me, "Well, I'm gonna whittle you down to a lot less than that." Spivey said, "Let's get out of here fast." Without looking back, we ran away as fast as we could.

After a while, Young Life gave me a van to transport kids and to take players to compete against other inner-city teams. One of the Harlem players was among the all-time greatest players in the history of inner-city basketball.

His name was Earl Manigault, a young man who was called "the Goat," based on the sound of his last name. Whenever "the Goat" walked onto the court, players would start chanting "Goat! Goat! Goat!"

Some say he was better than Michael Jordan, but Earl Manigault never played in the NBA. I played regularly against him and took him on trips when we played together against other inner-city teams.

Early on, however, Earl developed a drug problem. I heard that after he beat drugs, he returned to help the youth in Harlem. He died in 1998 at age 53.

There was a movie about him called "Rebound," in which Kareem calls him the greatest basketball player he's ever seen. I would agree.

CHAPTER 3

'We all know who you are'

SOME OF THE YOUNG LIFE VOLUNTEERS and I ended up taking a group of 32 young boys and girls from the Projects, including some basketball players, on a lengthy field trip to Frontier Ranch, a Young Life camp in Buena Vista, Colorado.

Most of them had never been out of New York City before.

We traveled by train and by bus, and many lives were changed that week through a tremendous amount of fun and the preaching of the Gospel of Jesus Christ. A while later, I took a similar-sized group of kids to a Young Life Camp in Minnesota. Once again, we had great fun and many lives were changed.

Toward the end of that summer my friends asked if I still wanted to go to the Latin Concert. I said, "Yeah, for sure!" There were some 30,000 people there and from my vantage point, I was the only white guy.

A man who introduced himself as a postman approached me and said, "I know who you are. We all know who you are, and you're safe here."

It was a very moving moment.

Through a combination of the crowded living conditions, late nights and playing ball constantly, I was getting worn out and experiencing what I now realize was culture shock.

About two weeks before we left for home, Bill Westphal and I moved into Harv Ostdyck's home in New Jersey. Harv, who was New York City's Young

Life area director, loaned us his car and we commuted back to New York from his home.

After a long day in the city, Bill and I were driving back in the evening on the New Jersey Turnpike. Bill had been ragging me a lot about my driving, using heavy doses of sarcasm.

I got so angry I pulled over, got out of the car and threw the keys as far as I could. I told him, "You don't like my driving? Go find those keys and you drive." Bill responded, "Great, what're we gonna do now?"

Somehow, we found the keys and I still drove home.

After we settled into our room, we had a good conversation about how sarcasm affects people differently, and we made an agreement not to use it on each other.

Bill and I got close to two good high school players named Pop Green and Perry Elliott.

While we were still in New Jersey, we contacted Don Williams and asked if Hollywood Pres could sponsor them with housing so they could attend Los Angeles City College.

They agreed, so it was set that they would live in a house on the campus of the church.

PART 6

USC senior year

CHAPTER 1

The difference between pain and injury

As a junior at USC, before I went to Harlem, I had averaged 16 points a game. As a senior, I averaged 25.5 for the season. I averaged 28.7 in the Pac-8, which was a record for years. I had become a player who could draw fouls and score from anywhere, plus add points from the free-throw line.

Without a doubt, that summer was the beginning of a whole change in my life, as a player and as a believer in Jesus.

The weekend before the Pac-8 season began, we played Vanderbilt, which had 6-11 All-American Clyde Lee, in the semifinals of the Los Angeles Invitational Tournament.

Early in the game I went up for a rebound, and as I came down with the ball, Clyde came down on my back. I landed with my ankle twisted with all of his weight on top of me.

The ankle was sprained severely, but I continued playing through the pain, and went on to score over 30 points. After the game, which we won, my ankle swelled up like a grapefruit. I was in so much pain that night I hardly slept.

The following night we played our crosstown rival, UCLA, coached by John Wooden. I told Coach Twogood that I wanted to play. I took something for the pain and played, but only at half-speed, dragging my foot around. We lost, which was one of the eight times we lost to UCLA during my entire college career.

I had a third-degree sprain, and on Sunday after the UCLA game, I began physical therapy. I met with the trainer, Jack Ward, and he had me go into a hot whirlpool for three minutes. He then slid a neoprene sleeve over my toes and the ball of my foot, and I placed my foot into a bucket of ice for three minutes.

I repeated the entire process two or three times a day.

Jack then taught me something that I would use as a player, and later throughout my coaching career. He told me to walk without a limp and keep full range of motion, because rehabilitation would take a lot longer if my range of motion was lost.

After five days of rehab, I was 90 percent healed, and able to resume practice.

Over the course of my life, I've had 31 surgeries along with a whole lot of other physical challenges. Still, I've always healed quickly. I've tried to keep my full range of motion with every injury, and I believe that Jack Ward was very wise in teaching me the difference between pain and injury, and how to deal with both.

After the ankle injury, our first Pac-8 game was against Washington. I scored 45 points, which remains a USC record to this day. I also went 21-for-21 from the free throw line, which also remains a Pac-12 record.

I was shooting a lot of free throws each game and making 80 percent of them. As I mentioned earlier, playing in Harlem taught me to make and take contact. This built upon the foundation I had been given by coach Abe Androff. Whenever I've gotten into slumps in basketball or crisis in life, I've always returned to foundational principles.

The weekend after playing the Washington schools, we played Oregon. The game was played at McArthur Court, an old, rickety arena known as "The Pit" because fans were so close to the action. There were two Oregon football players who had played at my high school behind the stands of our bench, razzing me.

By then I had learned not to let such distractions affect me.

Jim Barnett, who ended up being a first-round draft pick for the Boston Celtics, was a tremendous player at Oregon. Years later, we became teammates on the San Diego Rockets and later, we played together for the New Orleans Jazz.

He loved telling this story.

According to Jim, John Brockman, the 6-10 center for Oregon, was talking trash in the locker room about stopping me. By halftime it seemed he was right, since I had only 8 points. The crowd was really on me.

Brockman went into the locker room and declared, "Now I'm going to take care of Block in the second half."

Boy, was he surprised at what happened next.

CHAPTER 2

Totally block out the negatives

EVEN THOUGH I PLAYED only 15 minutes in the second half, I scored 36 more points, for a total of 44, including one play where I shot a turn-around jump shot and Brockman was right on me.

I leaned back as far as I could, and he hit my elbow while trying to block my shot. I was in the air when I was fouled, so I shot the ball just before landing flat on my back. Miraculously, the ball went in. After the first two weekends of Pac-8 play, I was averaging nearly 40 points a game.

I believe that God gave me the gift to compartmentalize things when needed. Somehow, I was able to block everything out, even Coach Twogood, who was very intense and yelled at us at practice and in games, which I couldn't stand.

Technically, he was a very good coach with a good basketball mind, but he coached by putting players down with sarcasm when they made mistakes. There was little encouragement or inspiration.

My goal was to get into the NBA and no coach or anybody else could stop me from getting there. I knew I couldn't do without a coach, so I decided to learn from Coach Twogood's positives and totally block out his negatives.

Once, in the middle of my senior year season, Coach Twogood came to practice in a bad mood. During a half-court scrimmage toward the end of practice he yelled at me, "Block, you're nothing but a big pussy." I calmly replied, "Coach, you know that's not true."

He didn't say another word and practice was soon over.

I stayed behind to work on free throws and then walked downstairs to the locker room. Coach Twogood had waited for me at the bottom of the stairs. With tears in his eyes, he said, "John, that was the worst thing you could have said."

It was obvious he was upset with what he had said to me, and he left without another word.

I liked Coach Twogood personally, but not how he coached. He gave me the opportunity to get a college education and to get drafted into the NBA. He had designed an offense that, in some measure, featured me. After my senior year, he retired from coaching.

About six years later he passed away with cancer just before his 65th birthday. His wife Eleanor called me soon afterward and told me his last words were, "I wish my two Johns were here."

She said he was referring to All-American John Rudometkin, who helped recruit me to USC when I was a senior in high school — and to me.

By the end of Pac-8 season I had averaged 28.7 points, which was a record for a long time until Reggie Miller broke it with 28.8. Kareem actually averaged the same number of points as me, but he had played one less game.

After the season, I was selected to represent the west in the College All-Star game in Lexington, Kentucky. I was really looking forward to it, but had twisted my ankle and was not at full speed. I played limited minutes and was less than stellar. My roommate for my stay in Lexington was Jim Barnett.

Little did we know that we'd be teammates and roommates in the NBA.

CHAPTER 3

Terrible blisters on my soles

SOON AFTER THE ALL-STAR GAME I was approached by Chris Severn, who had a prototype basketball shoe made by Adidas.

It was the first leather basketball shoe, and Chris asked me to try it out and make some suggestions on improving it. I used to drag my foot sometimes, as many other players did, when going in for shots and would wear out the toe of the shoe.

For that reason, a rubber shell toe was developed.

That shoe would eventually become the famous and now fashionable Superstar Shell Toe. I played in that shoe the entire summer.

My rookie year in the NBA, players were all playing in canvas shoes. I had to play in Converse All Stars when training camp began. Those shoes gave me terrible blisters on my soles because of all the movement of my foot within the shoe. The leather Adidas prototype kept my foot in place, and there were no more blisters.

That shoe was perfect for me. The next year I was with the San Diego Rockets, and we were the first team to play in the new Adidas shoe. I received plenty of shoes, but was never paid to wear them.

This gave birth to the Adidas "Superstar," which was developed from that prototype in 1970. Kareem was then signed to wear the shoe, becoming the first NBA player with a shoe contract.

Kareem and I were talking a few years ago and I told him I was the first player to wear the Adidas shoe, and he said he thought he was. I reminded him that I was wearing the Superstar even before they had named it. But he was definitely the first one to sign a shoe contract wearing that shoe.

Around that time, Bill Bradley, the Princeton All-American and Rhodes Scholar who later became an NBA Hall of Famer and then U.S. Senator, contacted me. He was visiting Los Angeles and asked me to take him to the best places to play pickup ball in the area.

We had a great time.

Bill, who was traveling around the country, playing against the best competition he could find, invited me to travel with him. I really wanted to, but I knew I couldn't commit to the time it would've taken.

PART 7

NBA: Lakers

CHAPTER 1

'Where do I sign?'

IN 1966 THE LAKERS DRAFTED ME in the second round of the NBA draft.

In 1966, the Lakers selected Jerry Chambers of Utah, the No. 1 scorer in the nation, as their first-round pick, followed by Hank Finkel of Dayton and myself in the second round, then Minnesota's Archie Clark in the third round.

As it turned out, Archie became the best player of all of us.

After the draft, general manager Lou Mohs made an appointment with me to meet in his office to talk about an NBA contract. I asked Don Williams to come with me because negotiation wasn't part of my thinking at the time.

All I wanted to do was play.

Lou said, "John, we're prepared to offer you $10,000 and a $1,000 signing bonus." All I said was, "Where do I sign?"

The school year was over when rookie camp began, but I got pneumonia and couldn't participate. Because I missed rookie camp, Fred Schaus, the Lakers head coach told me, "We're running youth clinics for six weeks around the city and I want you to be there."

I was a center in college but was going to be what the NBA now calls a power forward. I had to learn to pass and dribble for that position, so Coach Schaus wanted me to demonstrate ball handling and dribbling at the clinics.

He would have me come to the clinics early where he taught me ball handling and dribbling drills that I would teach later that day. The other rookies along with veterans like Jerry West, Rudy LaRusso, and Leroy Ellis also attended the clinics.

After the morning clinics, I'd usually play beach volleyball and in the evening I'd play pickup basketball.

When official practice began in September, there were veterans from last year's team along with drafted rookies and free agents trying out for the team. When the exhibition season began, which was about 15 games, we traveled all over the Western states.

The Cincinnati Royals, coached by Jack McMahon, traveled with us for many of those exhibitions. They also had a lot of players on their pre-season roster. Before each exhibition game we would play rookie games, and I excelled in them.

At that time, veteran NBA players would mentor rookies by sharing their wisdom of life and how to best play their position. Rudy LaRusso became my roommate when we traveled, and one of the first things he told me to do was to closely watch the great Jerry West — how he practiced and how he played.

During the preseason, I watched West do specific drills before and after practice to improve his game. I saw how focused he was and how hard he worked on every drill. Jerry, who came in first in all our sprints, also taught me some of the jump-shot drills that I still teach to this day.

Rudy also told me, "When you're on the bench, don't be a spectator or a cheerleader, be a student. Watch the great players that are in your position and watch me."

LaRusso was one of the toughest players I've ever been around. I learned a lot about toughness and aggression from him. On a personal note, Rudy advised me to take my time getting married and not have kids until late in my career. He said that all the travel and intensity you bring home makes it hard to raise kids.

Margie and I didn't get married for another couple of years and we had our first child, Allison, five years later. Two years after that, I retired.

Rudy was right.

CHAPTER 2

They were going at it

WE STARTED MY rookie season with a road trip to New York.

It was the second game of my career, and we were in the old Madison Square Garden, playing the Knicks, who had an unbelievably great team.

Willis Reed was a monster player for the Knicks. His teammate was shooting a free throw in front of our bench, and LaRusso was next to Reed, trying to keep him from getting a rebound, which in basketball lingo is called "blocking out."

I watched LaRusso closely all the time and I saw him aggressively hit Reed, which precipitated a fight. They were going at it and moving toward our bench when, for some stupid reason, I jumped off the bench and grabbed Reed from behind.

In the midst of the action, I couldn't tell if he had thrown me off or if I had been pulled off, but suddenly he turned around and threw a left hook that I never saw coming. I was knocked backwards, but did not fall.

When I was taken to the locker room the doctor said, "You've got to see your face!" He put me in this barber chair, and swung me around to see myself in the mirror. My nose was in front of my left eye.

He said, "This is really gonna hurt, but I have to put your nose back in place."

He was right. It hurt.

The next day I flew back to San Diego and happened to see a headline in the *LA Times* sports page that was something like, "Big Brawl, Block Gets Hurt." My teammates razzed me saying, "You'll do anything to get into the papers."

I went to Daniel Freeman Hospital, where they removed part of my septum and told me that if that happened again, they would have to restructure my nose. I had driven my brand new '67 Chevy Camaro to the hospital.

After leaving it in the parking lot overnight, I went to get my car and found it up on milk crates. My hot, custom-made rims and tires had been stolen. I loved that car. It had a 350-cubic inch engine and I had beefed it up even more, plus converted the transmission to four-on-the-floor.

It was a serious machine, and at the time I was a real hot-rodder. When I was travelling, I told Margie she could drive my car as much as she wanted. Oh, how she loved that.

Toward the end of that summer, my insurance company cancelled my insurance policy on the Camaro because I had been pulled over for three speeding tickets and crashed it once.

A friend of mine would drive my car to Forest Home Conference Center while I went with another group. He didn't show up because the car had backfired, caught fire, and was totaled. The only way I could get insurance after that was to buy a slower car.

I ended up with an International Harvester Scout. It was a four-banger (four-cylinder engine) that couldn't go much over 65 mph. When I moved to San Diego, I drove it back and forth to Los Angeles to see Margie whenever I could.

CHAPTER 3

Three large cups of warm water

MANY OF THE PLAYERS on the teams I've been on played cards. I was playing Hearts one late evening with Elgin Baylor, Walter Hazzard, and Gail Goodrich.

The loser of each game had to drink a cup of warm water. I'd been winning until they ganged up on me and I lost three straight games. So, I drank three large cups of warm water. I didn't realize what that meant until I tried to sleep. I was up going to the bathroom all night.

My teammates really got the rookie good.

Our per diem was only about ten bucks a day, but one evening, LaRusso, Baylor and West took me down this alley in Cincinnati where I ate baby back ribs for my first time. I'll never forget it, and they remain among my favorite dishes.

By the late '60s, our per diem went up to $18 a day. Heck, when we went to New York City, I'd spend half that on one hamburger.

When we traveled, we played a lot of games and hardly practiced. So, since I was a rookie and not yet playing in many games, I played very little basketball.

After a while, I approached Coach Schaus and said, "I think I figured out what it will take for me to be a better player. Would you consider me not traveling to the away games so I can work on my game? It will also save the Lakers some money."

He thought that was such a great idea that he had seven-foot rookie Hank

Finkel stay home with me to work on our games together for the rest of the season.

I was then able to link up with Rink Babka, a former USC basketball player who had won a gold medal in the 1960 Olympics for the discus throw. He taught me a program of strength training that really improved my game.

I worked hours and hours on my shot, outside moves, strength, and balance.

CHAPTER 4

A lot of pickup ball

WHEN I JOINED PICKUP GAMES at Hollywood Pres Gym, I was surprised to see Lew Alcindor there.

He was already the No. 1 player in the country and would eventually become known as Kareem Abdul-Jabbar. We ended up playing a lot of pickup ball in that gym, and, of course, Kareem dominated. He could dominate anybody at any time, but we all had a lot of fun together.

That led to adding pickup games on the adjacent outdoor court. Once word got around, the courts were packed with top players from all over the Los Angeles area, with college coaches showing up to watch the action and recruit.

Two of those players were high schoolers named Sidney Wicks and Curtis Rowe, who both became stars at UCLA and then in the NBA.

A regulation court is 50 by 94 feet, but the entire Hollywood Pres gym was only about 40 by 70 feet. The wooden backboards were just a couple of feet off the wall.

Dunking had been outlawed by the NCAA, because of Lew Alcindor. We also didn't allow it because it would break the backboards. The competition was fierce because of the long wait if your team lost. Halfway through our games, I'd stop and gather the players around the court and present a story about Jesus.

Toward the end of the school year, we decided to have a retreat and a basketball tournament at Forest Home with most of the players who attended the open gym at Hollywood Pres. We were able to use the gym at Redlands High, about a half-hour down the mountain from Forest Home.

We also flew in Bo Nixon, the Young Life director from New York's Lower East Side. In the evenings he would share the gospel. He related well to the players, and the tournament was outstanding.

CHAPTER 5

Young pimps and drug dealers

AFTER MY ROOKIE SEASON, I moved into an apartment in Los Angeles, near the USC campus. Don Williams introduced me to an 18-year-old named Danny Howe, who had come to know Jesus.

Don asked me if Danny could move in with me and my friend Paul Bowen so that I could disciple him. Danny was on probation and his probation officer told me that he had been among the most notorious young pimps and drug dealers in Los Angeles.

His dad started him doing and selling drugs when he was 8 years old. By the age of 18 he had done about every illegal thing there was. He had been stabbed many times and had a lot of scars to prove it.

By the time we met, he had given up most everything except "uppers." I would see him down 15 or 20 pills at once without it seeming to affect him. He was multi-talented and had taught himself to play the French horn like a professional. His handwriting was like beautiful script.

We spent a lot of time talking about Jesus, praying together and reading the scriptures.

Danny located a 1938 Packard touring car owned by an older lady. It had been parked in her garage for years, yet still ran like new. Even the radio worked. Danny said I could buy the car for $500. I bought it and used it for transporting young people to the Salt Company, the coffee house we helped start at Hollywood Pres.

Two years later, I found out that I could've sold that car for $30,000, but I ended up donating it to the church.

Before I went back to San Diego to start our preseason with the Rockets, Danny told me he was going to break parole and put himself back in jail. He said that everywhere he went people were trying to pull him back into his old life and that he didn't think he could stand up against it.

I'm not sure what he did to break parole, but after a time in jail, he was released to Teen Challenge.

He wrote me a letter saying that he appreciated what I had done for him, that he didn't have long to live, and looked forward to seeing me in heaven. It wasn't much later when I heard he was found dead in the front yard of his Teen Challenge apartment.

He was only 20 years old, and the autopsy said his body was like that of an 80-year-old. He had abused his body to the point that he died of old age.

PART 8

NBA: Rockets

CHAPTER 1

It entered my dreams

IN 1967 THE NBA added two new expansion teams, the San Diego Rockets, and the Seattle Supersonics. Each NBA team got to freeze five players, and the rest of the roster was available for the draft. I was drafted by the Rockets.

The summer before reporting to San Diego, I played in a Professional Amateur Summer League (Pro-Am) at Cal State Los Angeles. It was great fun and great competition.

Mack Calvin, who was playing for USC, was on that team. He was a prolific point guard who went on to have an excellent ABA and NBA career. I scored a lot of points each game because of Mack's passing. If I was running the floor on fast breaks, which I loved to do, he passed me the ball in the right spot every time.

We had such good chemistry, I would have loved playing with him my entire career.

I didn't know anyone in San Diego, but during my senior year at USC, Pat Harrison was a sophomore who became an All-American baseball player. He was in our athletes' bible study, led by Don Williams.

Pat had grown up in San Diego and his family still lived there. He asked his parents, Harry and June, if I could stay with the family until I got settled and found my own place. They said yes, and said they had two seven-foot bunk beds, which suited me perfectly.

I moved in with the family including Pat's brothers Chris and Mike, who were both good baseball players. I slept on the top bunk, and Mike was on the lower bunk. I was so immersed in basketball that it entered my dreams.

Once during my sleep, I jumped from the top bunk and landed on my knees, waking up everyone in the house. It didn't take long before I became part of the family, and they invited me to stay.

As unusual as it was for an NBA player to do so, I ended up living with the Harrison family for two years until I got married. They treated me like I was their own son, even coming to all my games as a family. They were a Christian family, and I went to church with them whenever we didn't have games on Sunday.

When I got to San Diego, I negotiated my contract and got a good raise. Our preseason camp was held at Cal Western University in Point Loma. I had no idea then that I would one day become the head coach on that campus which later became Point Loma Nazarene University.

During preseason camp, the team stayed at a hotel in Mission Valley.

My roommate was Dave Gambee, who was an eight-year veteran player from the Philadelphia 76ers, which had just won the NBA championship. He asked me if I would be interested in learning to play the guitar.

He bought a five-string banjo, and I bought an acoustic guitar. We found a good guitar and banjo teacher who taught us how to play bluegrass music together. We took our instruments to away games where we practiced, and I also practiced at home.

In time, I got into country, gospel, and Johnny Cash. I loved playing Cash's songs, especially "Dirty Old Egg Sucking Dog." Along the way, I'm sure the Harrison family really got tired of me practicing Johnny Cash songs.

During the regular season with the Rockets, I was the leading scorer and rebounder, averaging 20.2 points and 11 rebounds a game. Years later *Sports*

Illustrated noted that I had the second highest increase in scoring from one year to the next in NBA history.

It was a big year for me, and it was exciting to play against the Lakers and against my mentor, Rudy LaRusso, who was now with the San Francisco Warriors.

He had taught me well.

CHAPTER 2

Shattering my metacarpal

DURING MY CAREER, I played with 15 Hall of Famers, and against some of the top 50 players of all time. Some have called it the Golden Age of Basketball.

One of my most memorable moments in the NBA occurred that first year with the Rockets. We were in a four-team doubleheader in Philadelphia. Our opponent was the Boston Celtics, led by one of the greatest defensive players of all time, the legendary Bill Russell, who was guarding me.

It was early in the season, and he hadn't seen me before so he didn't know what I was capable of. With my first-step quickness and long strides, I was really good at driving to the basket. I was out in what is now the three-point line area, made a move and drove around Russell.

He went up to block my shot and I dunked on him with two hands. I remember so clearly going back up the court thinking, *I can't believe I just dunked on Bill Russell.* I never did it again.

My season was cut short after 52 games when I shattered a metacarpal bone on my right hand. I had two pins inserted, which were removed after it healed.

The original San Diego Rockets during the 1967–'68 team included Pat Riley, who was a first-round draft pick, along with Jim Barnett, Don Kojis, Jon McGlocklin, Toby Kimball and Johnny Green.

Green was at the end of his career and one day at practice he asked, "Anybody wanna bet that I can't dunk the ball ten times in 15 seconds?" We all chipped in and bet him. The coach had a stopwatch and Johnny stood beneath the basket.

He was only 6-5, but he went straight up, dunked the ball with his left hand, holding his right hand beneath basket. He dunked it 13 times in 15 seconds.

We were amazed.

Some of the players on that team would say that season was one of the most enjoyable of their careers, based on our camaraderie and an understanding that we were not expected to win many games.

CHAPTER 3

Bob Dylan and Jesus Christ

AFTER THE SEASON, I moved back to Los Angeles, where Don Williams introduced me to Bob Marlowe, who was a basketball guy, a guitar player and a singer who loved Bob Dylan.

He had learned to mimic everything Dylan did, so much that there was a point where you couldn't tell the difference between the two — at least in terms of their music.

Many of us thought it would be great to have Bob sing some Dylan songs and Don would then preach the gospel using Dylan's lyrics. Fliers went out all over the Hollywood area, reading: "Bob Dylan and Jesus Christ." The Hollywood Pres church sanctuary was jam-packed.

It went so well that people wanted Bob to continue playing after the service. So, from there he went to sing in a smaller area where people sat around enjoying the music. Out of those evenings came the vision for a coffee house called the Salt Company.

Bob put together a musical group of the same name, the Salt Company, based on the words of Jesus about us being salt and light.

The church eventually gave us the upstairs of a building to convert into a little coffee house. I oversaw the construction, and we decided to decorate it in a Western motif.

A nearby rancher said we could take as much of his old barn wood as we wanted, to use for the interior of the coffee house. We built a Western bar and served coffee, sarsaparilla, and other soft drinks.

We opened the Salt Company in the summer of 1968. Some incredibly talented musicians played there, some of whom would become big stars of Christian music, including Dennis Agajanian, Larry Norman, and Randy Stonehill.

The launch of the Salt Company was part of the genesis of what became the "Jesus Movement." We went to the streets and the beaches, did concerts and a lot of people came to know the Lord Jesus as a result.

During that time, I was playing pickup games at Hollywood Pres gym and spending time with Pop Green and Perry Elliott, two players I had gotten to know in Harlem. When I went to where they were staying, I was surprised to see Lew Alcindor there.

Lew was good friends with Pop and we ended up playing a lot of pickup ball together.

A few years later, he converted to the Muslim faith and changed his name to Kareem Abdul-Jabbar.

A year or so later, the house where Pop and Perry lived became a halfway house for those who had come to know the Lord. Many of them had endured bad experiences with drugs and other things. Though there were times we had no clue about what we were doing, we saw a lot of radical life changes.

It was the amazing ministry of God working through us.

The Salt Company was all about making relationships and relying on the Holy Spirit. Looking back, I see that God orchestrated the whole thing.

As it says in Proverbs, "Man makes his plans, but God directs his paths."

That same summer, Don Williams and a few of us rented a large house about three blocks from the boardwalk in Hermosa Beach.

I shared a room with a gay young man who Christ had radically transformed. By the time I met him, he was going up to Sunset Boulevard to share the Good News of Christ with gay individuals.

Most of my time was spent working at the Salt Company and practicing basketball while Margie traveled throughout Europe for the summer with her college roommate. The previous summer I had been living with a pimp and drug dealer. That summer I lived with a gay guy.

What was God up to putting such diverse people together? We were all sinners finding unity through Jesus.

There were several bubble-gum trading cards printed of me, and on the back of one of them, it says, "John manages a coffee house in the offseason."

CHAPTER 4

Just tell the truth

BACK IN 1967, the ABA (American Basketball Association) came into existence.

A year or so later, the NBPA (National Basketball Players Association) came into greater prominence as the NBA recognized the NBPA as the exclusive, certified labor union of the league's players.

As a result, NBA players' contracts became much more generous. Having averaged 20 points and 11 rebounds going into my third year in the league, I negotiated a *very* good contract with the Rockets.

As I had before, I negotiated my own contract. This time I was prepared to get a good raise.

Going into that season, Elvin Hayes was the Rockets' first-round draft pick from the University of Houston. A tremendous athlete and future Hall of Famer, he had a jump shot that simply couldn't be blocked. A relentless rebounder, he was similar to Bill Russell as a defender, and also led the league in scoring and rebounding.

What was great for me as an offensive rebounder was that Hayes would shoot his turnaround jump shots and usually bank them in. If he missed, I'd know where the rebound was going, and I'd hustle to get to those areas and grab it.

Early in my fourth year in the league, which was Elvin's second season, we were playing the Milwaukee Bucks in the Houston Astrodome. It was billed as a grudge match between Elvin and Kareem. When Elvin was with the University of Houston and Kareem was with UCLA, they played against each other in the regular season.

Houston won the game, partially because Kareem had injured his eye in a previous game. When they played again in the NCAA Tournament with Kareem, UCLA crushed Houston.

With all the hype, there were some 50,000 people in this huge football stadium, which set a record for NBA attendance at that time. The court was in the middle of the football field with no stands nearby. The crowd was so far away that the sound of cheers was delayed, as the only people near the court were media members, along with players and coaches.

It was like playing in a huge pasture.

It was a very close game, but Elvin had trouble guarding Kareem and fouled out at the end of the third quarter. Coach Hannum put me in at center to guard Kareem for the rest of the fourth quarter. I was very aggressive in guarding him.

Much of what I did would probably be considered outside today's rules, but the referees didn't call any fouls on me. Kareem became very angry and had only scored two free throws in the quarter. Toward the end of the game, I aggressively held him near the basket.

When the referees didn't call a foul, he came at me like he wanted to fight, cussing me out, calling me racist names. We lost that game, and I knew the reporters had heard what Kareem said to me.

Realizing they were going to ask me, I asked Coach Hannum how to deal with it. He said, "Just tell the truth." When the reporters asked if Kareem had said what they thought he said, I replied, "Yeah, he did."

Not long after that, Kareem and I crossed paths in an airport and he approached me, saying something to the effect of, "I know you were just doing what you needed to do, and the referees weren't calling it. I got really angry. I'm sorry."

He's a very private, quiet person, highly intelligent and humble, especially considering his super stardom. When I was with the Bucks, Kareem and I had some good discussions about many things, including our different faiths. We've always respected each other and that's only grown over the years.

CHAPTER 5

Was I really that nervous?

WHILE THE ROCKETS still had a losing season, we had improved to the point of making the playoffs. In the first round we were to play the Atlanta Hawks.

Coached by Richie Guerin, the Hawks had Lou Hudson, Bill Bridges, Zelmo Betty, Joe Caldwell, the same Joe Caldwell who jumped over me at Arizona State my sophomore year.

In the first half I was going up for a layup and got undercut by Walt Hazzard. That means he went low as I was in the air, and it flipped me so that I landed on my wrist. I was in pain when I shot my free throws.

In the second half, Bill Bridges intentionally fouled me while I was going for another layup. That knocked me to the ground, and I again landed on the same wrist. This time, the pain was too much, and I was out for the game.

We lost by two points and my season was over.

When we got home to San Diego, X-rays revealed that I had broken the navicular bone in my wrist, the smallest bone in the body and hardest to heal. I was to be in a cast for months, but Margie and I had planned on getting married in six weeks and then taking our honeymoon in Kauai.

On May 17, 1969, we had a big wedding planned at Hollywood Pres's big sanctuary. However, our plans were interrupted by the sad news on April 3rd that Margie's mother had passed away from a massive brain hemorrhage. After the funeral, we decided on a smaller wedding.

We invited Don Williams to officiate the ceremony at the Hollywood Pres chapel.

On the day of the wedding, Bill Westphal, Bob Marlowe, Jim Ferguson and I — wearing a cast on my arm — played quite a few games of two-on-two basketball in the church gym. Then we set up the volleyball court and played a few games.

After showering at the gym, I picked up my electric shaver and fumbled it into the toilet. For some reason, I immediately flushed the toilet. Was I really that nervous?

As a married couple, Margie and I moved to an apartment in Hermosa Beach near the ocean and some well-known beach volleyball courts. Paul Westphal was still in high school and lived nearby in Redondo Beach. Every day, we played volleyball on the beach and indoors, so much that I needed a new cast every few weeks.

We played a lot of H-O-R-S-E, a basketball game with two players each having to match the shot of the other. A player wins by making more matching shots, getting a letter in H-O-R-S-E whenever they miss a shot.

I could shoot only left-handed, so Paul shot only left-handed, which helped both of us get better with our off-hands. When Paul was in the NBA, one year he won the league's H-O-R-S-E competitions easily by using his left hand.

CHAPTER 6

Never used an agent again

BEFORE 1969–70 PRESEASON CAMP began, Margie and I moved into a large two-bedroom apartment that overlooked the San Diego Sports Arena.

Our friends, Greg and Cheryl Carlson, from the Hollywood Pres college department were newly married and were also moving to San Diego. We invited them to move in with us until they found a place for themselves.

We had been given a 12-week-old Shepherd and Samoyed-mix puppy that we named Brutus for a wedding present. He lived with us even though there were rules against it. He was just a little white fluff ball that we snuck in and out in big athletic bags.

I had been talked into hiring an agent to negotiate my contract. I figured it was going to go well, since I got a good raise for my first year with the Rockets. With Elvin leading the league in scoring and rebounding, I was still averaging 15.3 points and 9 rebounds per game.

After the agent talked with management, he told me they thought I had a bad year which didn't measure up to my previous year. He said they wanted to cut my salary or else not play for the Rockets. He talked me into taking less. I never used an agent again.

Veterans Johnny Egan and Larry Siegfried were added to the Rockets' roster for the 1969–'70 season. At 27–55, we had the worst record in the league. We started the season on the road and went one and one before losing two home games. We then went on an East Coast swing of five games, losing all of them.

The schedule was brutal. We played in Atlanta on October 29, in New York on the 30th, in Boston on the 31st, and in Detroit on November 1.

Now, I've been involved with basketball since I was 15, and I was a college coach for 23 years. So, I have great admiration and respect for the coaching profession and know how hard it is. One thing a coach is constantly doing is evaluating his team and players to get them more wins.

And for the most part, if they don't win, the coach gets fired.

That season Coach McMahon and Coach Hannum did everything they could to try to figure things out. They both kept changing the lineup and our playing time. As a result, we couldn't get into a consistency of roles, which made for instability and frustration, which led to losing.

CHAPTER 7

Don't Embarrass the Big Man

ONE OF OUR MOST MEMORABLE practices occurred after Coach Hannum took over the coaching position. This is what I call a "memory practice."

As a coach myself, I coached memory practices a couple times in all those years. What is a memory practice? No one will ever forget it.

Coach Hannum coached and motivated with peer pressure. That meant that if a player messed up in practice, the whole team or the team that the player was on suffered the consequences. The idea is to get players to understand that their individual mistakes hinder the team's success.

An example was Coach Hannum's five-player weave. He had us start at one end of the court, passing to a player on the move down the court and going behind him in weave pattern. The rules would be five passes down and layup, and four passes back, no dribbling, no fumbles of a pass, and no missed layups.

The players that mess up must continue doing the drill until they do it with no mistakes. In a scrimmage situation the rules would be no turnovers, no offensive rebounds, running a play incorrectly, and forgetting the play.

Also, all ten players had to be across half court before a shot was made. The team that broke a rule had to run five laps around the court. Sometimes a player or team would break under the pressure. Coach Hannum wanted to find out how far he could push the individual player or the team.

One day, "Big E," as Elvin was known, came to practice at the University of

San Diego gym intent on testing Coach Hannum. We started some practices with the three-man weave. Elvin made it clear that he didn't want to run and casually went through the motions.

In response, Coach Hannum declared that we'd keep running the drill until E started doing the drill correctly.

Fifteen minutes went by and we were dying out there, tongues hanging out, begging for E to help us out, but he didn't respond. After 30 minutes of running the three-man weave, Coach Hannum stopped practice. He had the team go outside the gym and told us to stay there while E stayed on the court with him.

After a few minutes, which seemed like an eternity, E came back to us and apologized to the team, saying he was ready to practice now.

As we were walking back out onto the court, Stu Lantz and I asked E what Coach Hannum said to him. I'll never forget his answer.

"That man's crazy! He was gonna kill me!"

E went out and practiced like there were seven devils after him. Our season ended at 27–55.

Management told Stu Lantz to play more one on one. He had played center-forward in college, but they wanted him to be a shooting guard. He was a great athlete, could jump out of the gym, and he was quick.

Most of that summer, Stu and I worked out daily together at the USD gym at 10 am. We would work on our shot and then play one-on-one for two hours.

Because of Stu being 6-3 and my being 6-10, we had special rules. No rebounding (advantage, me), two dribble maximum (advantage, Stu), any foul gets the ball back. If the ball goes out of bounds for any reason it was a turnover. We played mostly half-court, and when we wanted to stress ourselves, we played full-court.

We both benefited. I played a much quicker opponent, and he played a taller, more physical opponent.

In one workout Stu made a great move to the basket. I tried to block it, and he threw up a trick shot that went in. He said, "Oh, no!" He had embarrassed the big man. Next time he drove to the basket, he knew what was coming. I hammered him.

You don't embarrass the big man! We still laugh about that.

Margie and I moved into a house in La Jolla Shores in 1970, a block from the beach. Soon after moving in, we bought a couple of horses from Reverend Weddle, who owned a horse ranch and a small retreat center in Jamul, located in San Diego's rural East County.

We boarded our horses there, and even though it was an hour each way, we drove out to the ranch as often as possible. One of the cool things E and I did together was when we rode horses together in the July 4th Coronado parade dressed as cowboys with San Diego Rockets signs on our saddles.

Margie and I had no idea at the time that we would end up with a horse ranch and 17 Arabian horses.

CHAPTER 8

'Ya gotta love it'

IN 1970, RUDY TOMJANOVICH was our first-round pick and Calvin Murphy was our second-round pick, and both went on to become Hall of Famers.

Early in the season, I tried to catch an errant pass, came down awkwardly and significantly injured my back. I missed nine games because of that, but the team continued playing well. I came back, but was playing only a few minutes a game, and was playing poorly.

On January 1 and 2, we beat the Lakers away and then at home. We were leading the Lakers in our division with a record of 23–20 when we had a couple of days off. During that time, Coach Hannum injured himself waterskiing, causing him to miss a few games, which threw off our team's overall timing and rhythm.

From then on, we went into a tailspin, losing 16 of the next 17 games.

During that losing streak, there was a family-themed gift night at the San Diego Sports Arena. It was packed to near capacity with more than 13,000 fans. The coach put me in for the last minutes of the first half. I played poorly, turning the ball over, fouling, making all kinds of mistakes.

We'd been eight points up when I went into the game, and by halftime we were down by eight. The home crowd started booing when we went into the locker room.

When Coach Hannum put me in at the third quarter, the crowd booed, and from then on, the crowd booed me every time we played at home during that losing streak. I became the scapegoat, and I continued playing poorly.

During the losing streak, there was another memory practice in the San Diego Sports Arena. We scrimmaged against each other with games to six points.

Coach Hannum, reacting like many coaches do in the midst of a losing streak, wanted to make a statement to the team. He put in every rule he could think of. We played nearly an hour and didn't finish the game to six points. As punishment, he had us run at least 75 timed laps around the court.

We were frustrated and angry when a fight broke out between Big E and John Q. Trapp. Hannum, who was a big, strong guy, went in to break it up and was yelling for us to help. Nobody moved.

He finally got them apart but was still irate that no one helped him break up the fight.

In response, he sent the whole team running up and down all of the stairs in the whole arena. Coach Hannum was down on the floor doing one-arm pushups yelling, "Ya gotta love it," one of his favorite sayings. We played a game the next night and got drilled.

One day after practice, Coach Hannum asked me if I could stick around to talk. We met outside the USD gym overlooking the swimming pool.

He said, "John, I'm concerned you'll lose your career if we don't turn this around." He asked if I had any ideas, and I immediately replied, "Don't play me the next game. Start me the game after that, because they won't boo a starter."

That game was against the Cleveland Cavaliers, and I knew I would have a good game against them. I played well and we won that game, and 15 of our next 17 games.

Though I was not a consistent starter, I became a hero instead of a scapegoat, and my career was back on track.

PART 9

Oakbridge 1

CHAPTER 1

'Lord, help me with this'

ONE DAY, STAN BEARD, the Young Life director for San Diego, suggested that we should play some golf and get my mind off basketball.

As we walked down the seventh fairway, I asked Stan, "What's the biggest need for Young Life in Southern California?"

He replied, "We need a camp," and I said, "Okay, let's do it."

Over the next two years, I drove all over San Diego County looking for property for a camp and a horse ranch. One weekend Margie and I were driving toward Julian, out past Ramona, in the backcountry.

After we passed a sign saying, "Quarter Horses and Arabians for Sale," I immediately turned around, drove in and saw barns and sheds all painted in UCLA's colors of blue and gold.

As we drove down the driveway, we saw a young woman working outside a barn. When I asked if the owner was around, she said he wasn't. Back then, because I was an NBA player, I always threw out my name.

Within seconds of giving her my name, the owner of the ranch came out of the barn and said, "John Block, what are you doing around here?" It was Frank Costello, a man I had known through Rudy LaRusso.

Frank and Rudy were really close. Years earlier, LaRusso had told me about a company Costello had started and suggested that I buy stock in it. I did, and within a year it had multiplied so much I was able to sell the stock to pay for our honeymoon in Kauai.

I told Frank we were looking for property to build a camp and a ranch. He said, "Just today, I found out that the 80 acres behind me are for sale." He gave me the owner's name and number.

Turned out that the owner of the property also owned the sporting goods company that provided all the equipment for the San Diego Rockets.

I called him, told him what I wanted to do, and he said, "You got it." He dropped his price, we agreed on the terms, and Margie and I bought the 80 acres.

Stan helped get the Young Life board together to talk about building a camp. Every day, I drove out there and walked every square foot, praying, "Lord, help me with this."

As I walked and hiked, I envisioned the entire layout of the camp and ranch. I could see buildings for housing and meetings, courts that doubled for tennis and basketball, a soccer field, a sand volleyball court, and a half-sized Olympic swimming pool.

A man named Jim Woods owned a big Caterpillar tractor and lived in the area and did grading. Together we walked the property and staked out everything. We had an architect friend draw plans to take to the county.

The property was part of an agricultural preserve and many people said there was no way we would be allowed to build there. I went to the county planner, shared our vision with him, and told him that we needed his help. He helped me get through the entire process and a few months later we were approved to build.

PART 10

NBA: Bucks bound

CHAPTER 1

A spaceship on a pedestal

DURING MY NBA CAREER, I played for the Los Angeles Lakers, the San Diego Rockets, the Milwaukee Bucks, the Philadelphia 76ers, the Kansas City-Omaha Kings, the New Orleans Jazz, and the Chicago Bulls.

From the time of our marriage in 1969 until I retired as a player in 1976, Margie and I moved from Hermosa Beach to San Diego, then to La Jolla, then to Houston, then to Milwaukee (twice within one season), then back to San Diego, then to Philadelphia, then to Kansas City and back to San Diego twice.

Then we went from San Diego to New Orleans, then to Chicago. Then, San Diego to Chicago and back. That's 13 moves in seven years.

During more than a half-century of marriage, Margie and I have moved 36 times. But, in a measure of stability, we've been in our current home in San Diego for 22 years.

All of which is to say that after spending four years with the San Diego Rockets, the franchise was suddenly sold by owner Bob Breitbard to a group in Houston, Texas.

Luckily for us, one of Margie's cousins owned a house in Houston that he rented to us. We still owned our home in La Jolla and moved some of our belongings, including my Ford Bronco to our new home.

Preseason camp was to begin on Sunday, September 18. We flew to Houston Wednesday and unpacked Thursday. On Friday I was picked up by PR staffer Bruce Binkowski for a meeting to negotiate my contract with the Houston Rockets management.

A good guy, Bruce had been with the San Diego Rockets as an administrative assistant and moved to Houston with the team, so we already knew each other.

We went to a building that looked like a spaceship on a pedestal. When we got to the conference room, I was surprised to see multiple people there. There was an owner, the general manager, the coach and the trainer. I thought this was a weird group to begin negotiation of my contract.

After the usual small talk, I was asked what I thought my salary should be. I asked for an amount that was so high for that time, they might consider trading me. They did not immediately respond.

When they asked me what I thought the team needed, I knew something was up. I told them the team needed a backup center because Elvin Hayes was playing too many minutes.

They asked me who I would suggest, and I asked who was available. They said, "Dick Cunningham from the Milwaukee Bucks." My mind flew to the thought, the Bucks just won an NBA championship and I could be traded there.

"He would be great! Just check with Pete Newell. When Kareem didn't play against us, Cunningham would kill us." Pete Newell was the general manager for the San Diego Rockets and wasn't moving to Houston.

The conversation ended soon after that exchange and Bruce took me back to our house.

The next morning, I got a call from the general manager of the Rockets saying I was traded to the Milwaukee Bucks for Dick Cunningham. They wanted me there on Sunday because preseason practice began Monday. I made arrangements for our stuff to be stored in Houston.

I flew to Milwaukee and Margie flew back to San Diego until I could find a place for us to rent.

That Monday, I signed a satisfactory one-year contract with the Bucks. After preseason was over, I found an apartment in Brown Deer, 20 minutes away from the arena.

However, when Margie arrived at our upstairs apartment with our dog, Brutus, it soon became apparent this wasn't going to work. The neighbors were noisy, the dog needed to go out a lot and so we moved to a new corner apartment within the complex.

The NBA contract stipulates that in a trade the team was responsible for transportation of pets. Margie and I had two horses that we called pets and the Bucks paid for them to move to Milwaukee.

Guess what? The NBA changed the standard contracts the next year to stipulate that NBA teams were responsible only for household pets when players got traded.

CHAPTER 2

Steak, baked potatoes, and veggies

THE BUCKS WANTED ME TO BE a power forward "banger," which meant I would need to gain some muscle and add to my 210 pounds.

So, I did something that was unheard of in that era — I worked with weights during the season. I bought a squat rack that doubled as a bench press rack and an Olympic bar with plates and put it in our second bedroom.

I put on 20 pounds during the season, nearly all muscle.

There was one avid Bucks fan, a butcher, who left a big box of steaks at our doorstep once a month, which helped me gain muscle. Thanks to him, my daily diet consisted nearly entirely of steak, baked potatoes, and veggies. That became my pregame meal for many years.

Now, of course, many NBA players have their own nutritionist.

The team was highly successful, even though there was some racial tension. The white guys hung together, and the black guys hung together, but those divisions disappeared the moment we hit the court.

Bobby Dandridge, who was black, was a tremendous player from Norfolk, Virginia. My wife and his wife connected, and she and Margie attended an all-Black church on Easter Sunday. After the season, before we started our drive back to San Diego, I was at a gas station when I encountered Dandridge.

He said, "John, I watched you closely all season, and also our wives together. You're all right." That meant a lot to me.

Many years later we played golf together in Norfolk, Virginia.

By the way, teammates don't have to like each other so long as they have a common goal. When you hit that court for practice or games, it's business. When you leave, it's your own life. The best situation, though, is when everyone *does* enjoy each other's company.

Many of us on that Milwaukee Bucks team agree that it may have been the toughest season we've ever had. The main reason was Coach Costello did not have an assistant coach.

In the early 1970s, Lakers coach Bill Sharman started the game-day ritual of team shootarounds. Because of that, Coach Costello started doing it, as did other NBA teams.

The only difference was that ours became full up-and-down court drills, along with shooting. After the shoot-around, we watched 16-mm game film of opponents.

It became a two-hour session, which is a long time for a game day. I figured out we had less than 10 days off from basketball the entire season. Not that I'm complaining because we went 63–19 that season, but it was just very challenging.

The highlight of the season for me occurred when the Lakers were on a 33-game winning streak and came to Milwaukee to play us in an afternoon game on January 9, 1972.

It was a showdown.

Anticipation began building the night before when we played Detroit and blew them out. I had 19 points that game. Afterward, we left the arena with great anticipation because the unbeaten Lakers were coming to town.

When I awoke the next morning, I sensed that this was going to be a great day and a great game. When I arrived at the arena and walked into the locker room, it was electric. Not a person on our team believed the Lakers could beat us.

There were going to be six Hall of Famers in the game. For the Lakers, it was Jerry West, whose image is the NBA logo, Wilt Chamberlain and Gail Goodrich. For the Bucks, it was Kareem Abdul-Jabbar, Bobby Dandridge, and Oscar Robertson.

I didn't start, as Curtis Perry, a strong rebounding force, started ahead of me.

When I came into the game late in the first quarter, I was pumped. There were over 30 million people watching on TV with Keith Jackson and Bill Russell calling the action. I was *in the zone.* I just knew where our team's missed shots were going, and I was in the right place at the right time to grab offensive rebounds.

We led at halftime, 51–45, and I had 10 points and 7 rebounds. When I watched the replay of the video of that game, I was amazed to hear ABC's Keith Jackson and Bill Russell interviewing Coach Sharman on the main topic — John Block!

I remained in the zone through the second half. I fouled out after 21 minutes, but not before scoring 17 points and getting 10 rebounds. In my entire basketball career, nothing compares to that game.

We broke the Lakers' streak, winning 112–105.

CHAPTER 3

Don't trick the Big Man

THERE WERE TWO HEALTH SCARES for me that season. One was when I got my eye scratched. That healed quickly, but the other was more serious. In a game I was on the free throw lane with an opponent shooting a free-throw, when my heart started racing and beating irregularly.

I was feeling faint and very weak. It was so bad that I left the game immediately. My heart rate was over 250 beats per minute! It was my first experience of atrial fibrillation.

When I went to the cardiologist the next day, he asked about my diet. I told him I was drinking a lot of iced sweet tea. He told me to stop, because the high quantities of sugar and caffeine were probably triggering a-fib. I quit immediately.

My a-fib didn't occur again until about 15 years later when I was coaching.

On March 1, we met the Lakers again on the University of Wisconsin campus in Madison.

I was coming off the bench and in the second half, I dribbled down the left side of the court, with only Wilt Chamberlain back to defend against me. Going in for a layup, I barreled toward Wilt and the basket.

I knew there was no way I could make a straight-ahead layup, so I had to trick him. As I went in for a left-handed layup, I shot the ball off the backboard to the other side of the rim, thinking I would get it quickly and score.

There was only one problem.

Wilt read my move and we both grabbed the ball at the same time. I don't know what got into me, but I grabbed Wilt's wrist with my left hand, pulled it down, and shoved the ball to the rim with my right.

To my amazement, the refs called a foul on Wilt, which he wasn't pleased about. As basketball fans know, Wilt never fouled out of a game during in his entire NBA career. He became irate and started to come after me. Fortunately, his teammates and the referees restrained him.

One of the refs called a timeout and told both teams to go to our benches. He came to Coach Costello and told him to have a substitute ready to come in for me after my free throws.

The ref told me, "Block, you better make your free throws." After I made my second one, I went straight to the bench and didn't play the rest of the game, thank God.

Toward the end of the season, Bucks general manager Wayne Embry called me in and told me the 76ers were interested in me playing for them the next year. Wayne asked me if it was okay for them to contact me. I said sure.

At the beginning of the season, Wali Jones, who had played for the 76ers, was traded to the Bucks for future considerations. The future consideration was that the Bucks would freeze five players and the 76ers could choose a player from the remaining players.

I told the 76ers that I'd be interested in playing for them, so I became the future consideration.

I signed a really good contract for the coming season.

That summer, a Milwaukee Bucks contingent consisting of Wayne Embry, Larry Costello, Lucius Allen, and I were invited on a goodwill tour. This was during the Vietnam War and we visited Armed Services bases and hospitals.

We traveled first-class in Air Force planes with a GS-15 designation, the equivalent pay grade of a colonel or captain. We went to Hawaii, Philippines, Guam, Okinawa, Tokyo and Taiwan. Margie met me in Japan, and we went to Taiwan together.

It was one of the most emotionally wrenching trips in my life, seeing so many soldiers injured and dying while we tried to encourage them.

PART 11

NBA: Sixers and Kings

CHAPTER 1

Playing a lot of Cribbage

THE 76ERS' PRESEASON CAMP was in Scranton, Pennsylvania. I drove from San Diego to Scranton and took along a younger friend of mine, Larry Burton. Larry wanted to drive up to Boston to hang out with Paul Westphal and his wife, Cindy.

Cindy and Larry had gone to high school together. He was then going to fly back to San Diego. We drove my Ford Bronco where I had set up an ice chest between the front seats with a towel over it that became our card table.

The trip took us four days, and we played over 200 games of Cribbage with one of us ahead by just a couple of games. I would end up playing a lot of Cribbage with my 76ers teammates.

The team management had done some screwy stuff including trading away some really good players. We started with a corps of veterans led by Bill Bridges, Hal Greer, Kevin Loughery, and Leroy Ellis, a former Laker.

Roy Rubin was the 76ers' newly-hired head coach from Long Island University who had never coached in the NBA. Let's just say that I learned a lot about how *not* to coach from him.

From the start, preseason camp was disorganized and we figured out early that it was going to be an up-and-down season, mostly down. Way down. We started by losing our first 15 games.

A few weeks into the season, we were in San Antonio playing the Houston Rockets. The score went back and forth, and Leroy Ellis and I were having good games. After regulation, we went into two overtimes and I played all 58 minutes.

With one second left and the game tied at the end of the second overtime, I was fouled in the act of shooting. I made both free throws and we won.

I was too exhausted even to celebrate what was our first win, but when I turned back to the bench, I saw Coach Rubin leap for joy from his seat. In the process, he tore a hamstring and got carried off the floor.

Meanwhile, I'd been hired as a spokesman for Coca-Cola and did a TV commercial that took place in the locker room. I had no idea how many takes it took to do a commercial. I thought playing basketball was tough, but following a script in front of TV cameras was torture.

Remember, I had been inherently shy. Another sponsorship came from a Buick dealership that gave me a car to use for free.

One weekend Margie and I drove that car to the Baltimore area to visit an Arabian horse-breeding farm owned by the Academy Award director, Mike Nichols. He toured us around his farm, and later we had tea and crumpets while discussing basketball and horses.

The NBA All-Star Game was coming up and I was named to the Eastern Conference team. Our last game before the break was in Baltimore. We were down at halftime, which was nearly always the case.

In the locker room Coach Rubin berated John Q. Trapp and told him to put on his warmups because he wasn't going to play the second half. I came out of the game in the fourth quarter and sat at the end of the bench between Q and Kevin Loughery, who was injured and not playing.

Q had a large Coke cup that he was drinking from, and asked me if I wanted any. Kevin said to me, "You don't want to drink that." It was bourbon and Coke.

I told Q, no thanks.

What saddened me most about that season is what Roy Rubin, I believe with the blessing of the front office, told Hal Greer in mid-season. He said Hal would never play again for the 76ers after that season.

One of the most engaging and professional players I've ever been around, Hal had been instrumental in winning an NBA Championship and was a future Hall of Famer.

I never heard him complain, even though we had a lot to complain about.

I loved competing with Hal, shooting free-throw line backboard shots, and playing cards on the bus and on plane trips, which he almost always won.

A class individual, he was once quoted as saying, "Each player should try to improve each game, each minute. Each time on the floor, you should try to learn something different."

That was the way I went about things. As a player and a coach, I don't believe it could be said any better.

By the way, Roy Rubin was fired around the All-Star break. Our record was 4–47.

CHAPTER 2

A Thrill and an Honor

BELIEVE ME, IT WAS AN HONOR to be selected for the All-Star Game, but I was realistic in knowing I'd been chosen from a team that was 4–47 at the break.

Not only that, the NBA had a long-standing policy that mandated the selection of at least one player from each team, a policy that ended the next season.

I played four minutes and scored four points, and it really was a thrill to compete against so many future Hall of Famers.

One of them was "Pistol" Pete Maravich, in the first of his five All-Star Games. At practice the day before, Pete exhibited some of his ball-handling and dribbling drills that he was famous for.

We couldn't believe the things he could do with a basketball. He was so far ahead of his time, so different in his style of play that the NBA culture wasn't quite ready for him.

During All-Star weekend, there were rumors of trades involving me and my teammates. Margie and I weren't happy living in Philadelphia and the team was awful, with a coach who, bless his heart, didn't know how to coach.

The day of the All-Star Game I had heard that Tom Van Arsdale and I might be linked to a trade with the Kansas City-Omaha Kings. At that time, my friends Toby Kimball and Don Kojis were playing for the Kings.

Right away, I went to the GM's hotel room and asked him about the trade. I told him that if it was possible, I was all for it.

Margie and I flew back to our apartment in New Jersey the next day and I went to practice. That morning, they fired Roy Rubin and hired Kevin Loughery as the new coach.

After a very tough practice, Loughery said to the team, "Don't anybody leave. We've made a trade and we don't want anyone to hear about it on the way home."

John Q. Trapp, who was sitting next me said, "It's me, I just know it is." I could understand that, since he had been sitting next to Kevin and me in a game drinking bourbon.

Kevin soon came in, looked at me and said, "John, can you step outside with me? The rest of you can leave." He said, "We've traded you to Kansas City for Tom Van Arsdale. They want you in Atlanta by tomorrow."

I got Tom's phone number and called him.

"Hey, Tom," I said, "Let's make this easy. I'm renting month-to-month and so are you. Let's just trade apartments. Leave your key under the mat and so will I."

Things worked out just fine. Margie flew back to our home in San Diego, and I went off to Atlanta where the Kings were playing.

CHAPTER 3

At the risk of being benched

When I arrived at the Kings' hotel, I went to visit my new teammates Don Kojis and Toby Kimball. They were in the room with Matty Goukas, who would be my roommate for the next year and a half.

Bob Cousy, the Boston Celtics great who became a Hall of Famer, was the Kings' head coach. I asked them how he was as a coach. "You'll see," they said.

At halftime we were up by 8 points and not playing particularly well. I didn't play at all.

When Coach Cousy came into the locker room, he was extremely irate. He said we were awful and put his fist through the blackboard. Then he put in rules for the second half that we had to abide by at the risk of being benched.

The major rule was no outside shots. Drives to the basket only. We did what he said and lost. His comment after the game was, "Now *that's* how the game is to be played."

We couldn't believe what we were hearing.

Many coaches who have been great players want their players to play like them. They want you to do exactly what the coach says, exactly the way the coach wants it done. They want total control because it's easier to coach that way.

Of course, it's also easy to let players just do what they want to do. There needs to be a balance between the two.

Usually, I can adapt to any philosophy and system that a coach teaches.

But it took me longer to adjust to Cousy's system that totally revolved around another future Hall of Famer, guard Nate "Tiny" Archibald.

The highlight for Archibald that season was that he led the league both in scoring and assists. Quite a feat. Tiny had the ball in his possession between 70 and 80 percent of the time.

That meant many of us had to fight to get position on the floor so that if Tiny had to pass the ball, we'd be there. He was so gifted at scoring from anywhere it was tough to get a read on offensive rebounds.

It was a tough, frustrating season.

I was glad it was over so that Margie and I could get back to San Diego.

PHOTO ALBUM 1

At age 2, I couldn't read yet, but I was fascinated by stories of Western lore. By the way, that's a sucker in my mouth, not a cigarette.

My dad is holding me, with his parents (at left) standing next to us, and my nephew below.

I'm all smiles with my sister Carol.

Me and my dad at our chicken ranch, and our dog whose name I can't remember because I was only 16 months old.

Though I had a short career as a boxer, I won an award and made my coach proud.

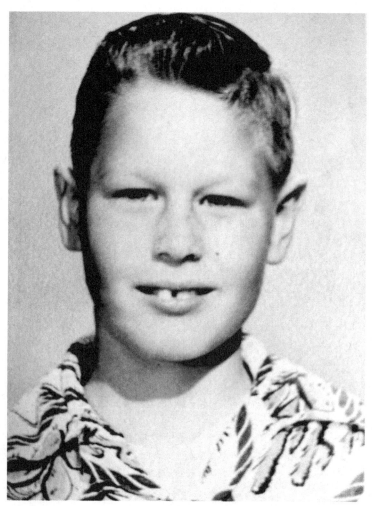

Yep, that's me at age 10, buck teeth and all.

In front of our Glendale home, I'm with my parents, Bill and Benny, and my sister Carol. My mother's given name was Zelpha. When she came to Los Angeles in her early 20s with three girlfriends from Kansas, they nicknamed her Benny because her hometown was Benedict, a small town in Kansas.

I'm a gangly 12-year-old Cub Scout, in front of our 1941 Cadillac.

My dad's Union Oil station in Montrose, about three miles from our home, where I started working at the age of 11.

I'm with my sister Carol and Rusty, our Irish Setter, taken on the 5-acre horse ranch in Canoga Park, where we lived for a few years.

My dad and me playing ping pong at a neighbor's home.

A "tall drink of water" shooting a hook shot in the Glendale High gym. As a junior, I was 6-8, 165 pounds.

Terrible form, but I cleared the high jump bar at 6-feet. It was my first-ever attempt on the first day of practice with the track team.

Margie (left) and my sister Carol with my hot '69 Bronco, which I drove everywhere, including countless long-distance trips.

Ready for my rookie season with the LA Lakers.

SAN DIEGO ROCKETS

JOHN BLOCK   6'-10"   FORWARD

My official San Diego Rockets mug shot.

I was a "long jumper," having already been fouled by the Suns' Connie Hawkins while making a reverse layup for the Rockets.

When I've got this big an opening to the basket, I'm home free.

My official Milwaukee Bucks mug shot, tough guy version.

*I didn't ever want to get in Wilt Chamberlain's way.
Note my Adidas shoes, the NBA's first-ever.*

SAN DIEGO ROCKETS
ST. LOUIS HAWKS
OCTOBER 17, 1967

SAN DIEGO INTERNATIONAL SPORTS ARENA

The official game program from the San Diego Rockets' 1967 preseason game against the St. Louis Hawks, played at Golden Gym on the campus of Cal Western University, now the site of Point Loma Nazarene University. In the photo, that's Seattle's George Wilson fouling me.

I don't think Hall of Famer Spencer Haywood is pleased with my grabbing defense.

Scene from the
free-throw line dur-
ing an exhibition
game between the
San Diego Rockets
and the Seattle Su-
personics. Seattle
Center Coliseum,
Seattle, Washington,
late 1960s

An artistic photo taken by celebrated Sports Illustrated *photographer Walter Iooss.*

Margie and I are looking sharp at a USC sorority–fraternity luau.

On our Wedding Day, May 17, 1969, I'm hugging Don Williams, who officiated the ceremony at Hollywood Presbyterian chapel. At left is my best man Bill Westphal, and at right is Bob Marlowe, my groomsman.

It's official! Margie and I are married.

We're all smiles after the wedding ceremony and reception. The next day, we were off to Kauai for our honeymoon. I'm hiding my right arm because it was in a cast.

Margie and I take a break during one of our many hikes in the High Sierras.

Toward the end of our cross-country camping trip, Jeff, me, Margie, and Allison stopped at the Grand Canyon's South Rim.

At left, my son-in-law Dave and Allison, with Asher and my daughter-in-law Leanna, my son Jeff, with Ezra and Corban in front. Taken at Mammoth Lakes village.

During the Bucks' win over the Lakers on January 9, 1972, breaking their 33-game winning streak, I'm pumped after hitting an outside jumper. A few days later, this photo ran in Sports Illustrated.

Chris Severn holds the prototype Adidas basketball shoe, similar to the version I helped him develop and then wore during my NBA career.

Margie and me enjoying the fall colors of Colorado's high country, 2021.

Our son Jeff (at right) with his family (left to right) Leanna, Asher, Ezzy, and Corban, at Convict Lake near Mammoth Lakes, summer of 2022.

Margie, Jeff, me and Allison at the summit above our Virginia Lakes cabin in the High Sierras. Margie's father helped build the cabin in 1943 and Margie and I have been going there ever since we met.

Rafting in the Smokey Mountains of Tennessee, during our nationwide tent camping trip.

The Salt Company Coffee House crew. I'm on the right, in the back row.

I was in charge of building the Salt Company, which included helping to design the coffee house and lots of demolition and disposal.

I don't know what else to say about this, except that it really is me, from my Salt Company days.

A sing-along with Bill Westphal (left), Bob Marlowe, Paul Westphal and me.

I have no clue why I'm wearing a suit with my arms crossed on the Salt Company stage.

PART 12

Travels with Margie

CHAPTER 1

Through an Artist's Eyes

THAT SUMMER, MARGIE AND I took a charter flight from San Diego to Frankfurt, Germany. We had 30 days to tour Europe. Our luggage consisted of one medium-sized Adidas bag and one double-wide sleeping bag.

We camped without a tent, stayed in hostels, *pensiones* (a small hotel with bed and breakfast), and inexpensive hotels all over Europe. We did that entire trip using the aptly titled book, *Europe on Five Dollars a Day.*

We rented a Volkswagen Beetle, which proved a challenge on the Autobahn because people frequently exceeded speeds of 100 mph. If we were passing a truck and saw a car in our rearview mirror, no matter how far back, we couldn't pass because the car would overtake us.

We planned to be in Rome for the Italian Open tennis tournament that our friend Stan Smith was playing in. We watched Stan's matches and then hung out with him and his one-time UCLA rival, the legendary Arthur Ashe.

I contacted Nancy Circelli Kominski, the mother of my former high school and Glendale College teammate, Mike Kominski. She lived in Rome and had become one of the most renowned art teachers in Europe.

After selling her art studio and packing her paintings, she moved from

Burbank, California to Rome without knowing the language or a single person there. When she checked into the YWCA in Rome, she asked if they had a teaching artist position.

An art teacher had just quit that day, so Nancy was hired on the spot.

She had developed a technique where students could finish a painting in one week that they were proud to hang in their home. The wives of many world leaders came to Rome and learned from her.

Her fame spread internationally and she ended up having one of the most popular TV shows in all of Europe.

Nancy set us up in a *pensione* just across from the Coliseum owned by one of her clients. What an experience to have Nancy show us Rome through an artist's eyes.

Leaving Rome by car was one of the biggest challenges of the entire trip. On certain days one-way streets changed directions. I knew how to leave town when the traffic flowed one direction, but when they were reversed, I kept going in circles.

I became so angry that I drove down the wrong way to get to a street I knew led out of town. Margie freaked out! We took the ferry from Italy to Greece where we slept on the beaches and visited all of the tourist attractions.

After leaving Greece, we drove into a small town in Yugoslavia. As we approached the town square, a bicyclist turned right in front of us and I hit him. We were in a communist country, and extremely concerned.

Thankfully, a policeman saw the whole thing. He knew we were Americans. In perfect English, he said, "Don't worry. He's going to be okay. Just keep going."

We drove into Dubrovnik, which was one of the most beautiful places we had ever been. It is a walled city that sits right on the Mediterranean.

Around noon, we stopped to eat cheese and crackers on a rocky outcropping overlooking the sea. We went into the water that was so clear we thought we were stepping into two feet of water, which was actually eight feet of water.

I heard the sound of a bouncing basketball, and went to see what was happening. A group of boys were playing, so I went over and joined them.

They asked if I played in the States and when I told them I was in the NBA, they were really excited.

I taught 'em a few things, and of course, I had to dunk for them.

It was an amazing whirlwind trip that we'll never forget. Up to this time of our marriage, my NBA career was also like a whirlwind.

PART 13

NBA: Kings and Bulls

CHAPTER 1

A Personality Conflict

AT THE BEGINNING OF THE 1973–74 SEASON, the Kings were playing an exhibition game in Michigan against the Detroit Pistons.

One of Coach Cousy's many rules was that our center, Sam Lacey, always took the ball out of bounds, which included when free throws were shot. There were seconds left in the third quarter, and a Detroit player was shooting a free throw. I glanced down court to see my roommate Matty Goukas unguarded.

I said to Sam, "I got this one," which meant I was going to take the ball out of bounds. He said, "Are you sure?" I said, "Yep." The player made the free throw and I took the ball out of bounds, throwing a baseball pass to Matty.

Problem was, the ball went off the side of my hand and sailed over Coach Cousy's head and into the seats.

Irate, Coach Cousy jumped off the bench and yelled for Ron Riley, "Ronnie, get in for Block." With less than 10 seconds left on the clock, I went to the end of the bench and Coach Cousy, standing, glared at me while the quarter ended.

He said, "Block, what in the hell was that?" As sarcastic as I could, I said, "Coach, that was a bad pass." The players had to restrain him from coming at me, but I just stood there as he shouted, "Block, you know Sam takes the ball out."

I responded by saying, "Yeah, and you could have just told me that."

He came at me again, and was again restrained by the players. I had balled up my fists and was ready for him. I obviously didn't play the fourth quarter.

After the game, I met with Stu Lantz, who was playing for Detroit. He asked me what was going on at the end of the third quarter. I told him and he was amazed that it was about me, because it was so out of character. That's the only time I've ever responded to a coach like that.

When I got on the team bus, I sat toward the front.

As he passed by me, Coach Cousy stopped and said, "I guess we have a personality conflict, don't we?" I said, "Yep, I guess we do."

We were 6–14 when we arrived in Boston to play the Celtics. The day before the game, Coach Cousy called a team meeting in Sam Lacey's hotel room. Once we were settled on the beds and floor around the room, Coach Cousy with tears in his eyes, said that he had resigned as head coach.

He then walked out of the room and we all cheered.

Draff Young, who had been the assistant coach, became the interim head coach. We had a close game with Boston and lost. After the game, Draff entered the locker room in tears apologizing to us for letting us down.

Someone spoke for all of us, saying, "Come on, Draff, you didn't let us down. You just now got the job."

What a season it was so far.

During one of our early home games against the Milwaukee Bucks, our center Sam Lacey was injured and unable to play. I started at the center position, which meant I would guard Kareem.

I took him outside so he couldn't guard me as well as he normally would have. I scored 26 points in 37 minutes and he scored 22 points in 43 minutes.

I was pushing and banging on him on defense when he turned to me and said, "Block, why don't you just give it up." Of course, I didn't. In the end, we got blown out by 34 points.

CHAPTER 2

Packing our stuff

A FEW GAMES LATER, Phil Johnson became the Kings' head coach. He had been the longtime assistant with Dick Motta for the Chicago Bulls, and he was a good coach. I liked him a lot, but didn't play well for most of the season under him, which was disappointing for both of us.

The next season when I was traded to the Bulls, I found that Coach Johnson ran all of the same plays as the Bulls did, and that his coaching tactics were exactly the same as Motta's.

Our team knew we weren't going to be in the playoffs, so Margie and I were got busy packing our stuff into our horse trailer for our move back to San Diego. We planned on leaving for San Diego the next morning after our last game, which was in Detroit.

All we had left to do was put our clothes into the trailer.

After our game, we flew back home to Kansas City, arriving around 1 am. The terminal where we disembarked the plane looked out to the large parking lot. As my teammates were getting off the plane, they asked me why Margie had the horse trailer hooked up to our Bronco, which I didn't know she had done.

Margie, who had packed all our clothes in the back seat, promptly told me that we needed to leave right then.

When I asked why, she said we needed to drive all night so we could stop by a ranch on the way in Wichita, Kansas, to see a mare we had the rare opportunity of buying. This was one of the most beautiful mares either of us had ever seen.

We ended up buying her and having her transported to our ranch in Ramona. We had fallen in love with that horse, and she became the foundation of our Arabian horse breeding venture.

I laugh when I think that we were out of the state before my teammates got to bed.

Because of the average year I had with the Kings, I knew I was going to be placed on the expansion draft list for the newly-formed New Orleans Jazz.

I got a call from Toby Kimball whom I had played with on the Rockets, Bucks, and the Kings. Both of us played the same position, but we were good friends, as were our wives.

When I answered the phone, he said, "I have the list of the players selected for the Jazz. Let me read it to you." He read his name and then down the list, my name.

He said, "I'll be damned if I'm going to play with you on another team," and slammed the receiver down.

I understood his frustration, and we remained good friends for many years.

PART 14

Oakbridge 2

CHAPTER 1

With a tractor and an auger

THAT SUMMER, ONE OF THE OWNERS and the general manager of the New Orleans Jazz came to meet with me at San Diego International Airport.

They had heard that I was involved in building the Oakbridge camp and a horse ranch, and seemed concerned that my heart wasn't into playing any longer.

I explained that I was working hard, staying in shape, and playing pickup games. I assured them that I'd be ready for the season, but I'm not sure that I convinced them.

Meanwhile, back at the ranch, I dug all the ditches for the electrical and water pipes using a "ditch witch." With a tractor and an auger, we installed over 3,500 linear feet of three-railed wooden fencing, cementing every post.

Over the years of building Oakbridge and the ranch, I was helped by many good friends, including Mike Dodd, who came out to help while he was playing basketball for San Diego State.

Later, Craig Knudson, who played basketball at my old high school and at San Diego State, was there to help, too. It was a lot of work and I was there every day.

Rick Jeffrey was a USC classmate who was involved in the college department at Hollywood Pres. His father, Eric, had been a USC track star in the 1940s. As a member of the church, Eric had closely followed my playing career, as well as my involvement in Harlem, and with the Salt Company.

After my summer in Harlem, he anonymously supported me with $50 a month during my senior year at USC. When he found out about my plans for Oakbridge and the ranch, he called to say he wanted to be a part of it. I told him I needed someone to look after my horses while Oakbridge was developing.

He said, "We're in."

First, I built a pad for a doublewide trailer, then he sold his home and his gas station, took early retirement, bought a doublewide trailer, and moved it onto the ranch property.

During the early years, Eric and his wife Janet took care of our three horses and worked diligently to build Oakbridge and the ranch. They were faithful prayer warriors, and he was like a father to me.

Margie and I had bought the property in 1973, then started construction on Oakbridge and the ranch in 1974. Four years later, we finally opened our first basketball camp. We had designed seven-foot bunk beds for basketball players that could be pulled out to become king beds, with the idea that the entire family could stay together.

Young Life and other church groups used it for weekend camping getaways.

The first fundraiser for Oakbridge happened to be scheduled for August 2, 1974, the same day that our daughter Allison was born, so obviously I was with Margie at the hospital.

Though Margie and I didn't know it at the time, we later learned that Allison's name means "Bringer of truth." She has been true to her name.

From the beginning, I knew that Allison was a gift from God. After she came home, I carried her to the beach. At the ocean's edge, I held her up and said, "Lord, Allison is yours. I dedicate her to you. Help us, Lord, to be good stewards of your daughter."

PART 15

NBA: Jazz and Bulls

CHAPTER 1

'Where am I going?'

WHILE MARGIE AND BABY ALLISON stayed in San Diego, I flew back to the Jazz's preseason camp, which began on September 15.

We were in two-a-day practices when I injured my quadricep doing a stupid charging drill. Meanwhile, Toby Kimball had injured his knee and after the season began, he declared he was retiring. I was just coming off the injury when Margie and Allison flew to New Orleans to our furnished apartment that had a month-to-month lease.

Four games into the season, I got a late-night call from Bill Berkta, the general manager of the Jazz.

His exact quote was, "We made a move that we think will help you and help us." I said, "Great, where am I going?" He said, "Chicago Bulls."

Immediately, I sat up on the edge of the bed and thought, that's great.

Berkta asked if I would mind having Dick Motta, the Bulls' GM, call me after we hung up. I said, "No problem." I was very excited because I knew their offense and that they were a very tough, hard-playing team.

Motta called me and said, "John, we're glad to get you because Chet Walker is coming off an injury and Bob Love is holding out on his contract," referring to the Bulls' two leading scorers. I asked when he wanted me to report.

He hesitated a bit, then said, "We're playing in New Orleans tomorrow night and we're bringing your uniform. You'll be playing tomorrow night."

So, I wore a New Orleans Jazz uniform one night and a Chicago Bulls uniform the next. It was after midnight when the deal was confirmed, and the newspapers didn't have time to print the story. As a result, there was no announcement made that I had been traded.

After arriving early at the arena, I went directly to the visitors' locker room when a security guard asked me where I was going. I said I was going to my new team. I got dressed and came out to shoot around before the game, wearing a Bulls uniform.

Knowing that I was a trickster at times, my now former Jazz teammates, Pete Maravich, Jim Barnett and Stu Lantz, thought I was fooling around. Nope, I'd been traded. But nobody knew it yet.

The game was close when Coach Motta put me in the game in the 4th quarter. Since I was familiar with New Orleans' plays, I had a couple of steals and rebounds, and we ended up winning.

CHAPTER 2

Things Weren't Working Out

ONCE AGAIN, MARGIE HAD TO CANCEL the lease on our New Orleans apartment, pack up and fly back to San Diego. Meanwhile, I flew to Houston, where I practiced with the team the day before we played the Rockets.

Prior to the game, when the team came onto the court to warm up, there was Margie in one of the front row seats. She flew there to surprise me and to see her relatives. I didn't start the first half, but I started the second half.

After that, I started the remainder of the games on that road trip. We went 4–2 and I averaged in double figures.

The team returned to Chicago and Margie stayed in San Diego until I could find a place to rent. I continued to start, averaging double figures until Bob Love settled his contract dispute with the Bulls. His first game back was against the Milwaukee Bucks.

I started the game, but played poorly and Love came in for me. From then on, I was the sixth or seventh man coming off the bench.

It was a difficult adjustment for me, and Coach Motta said it was okay and to settle down. I liked the way Coach Motta handled this veteran team. We had an eight-player rotation, and all of us knew our roles, when we were going to play and for how long.

For a player, there's no greater sense of freedom and security than knowing what your role is, which applies both to sports and life. When I became a coach, I adopted that philosophy.

At times during the season, I began having difficulty breathing on the court, but our team doctors couldn't figure out what was wrong.

As I look back, I realize it was stress-related. It got better, but I only played in 54 out of our 82 games that year. My early success was overshadowed by less and less playing time, but the team played well and we made the playoffs.

We lost in the semis that year against the Golden State Warriors, who went on to win the NBA Championship.

Prior to the 1975–'76 season, I went to camp unsigned, without a contract. I had a conversation with Coach Motta about my role and mentioned that I could play center and power forward, if needed.

In an exhibition game, I was on a fast break, racing down the middle of the court when point guard Norm Van Lier was dribbling down the sideline, and passed me the ball.

I was at the top of the key, near the free-throw lane when he threw it behind me. I pressed on the brakes and slipped on some sweat near the free-throw line and went down hard on my tailbone. I knew I was hurt, but I kept playing.

Things weren't working out the way I thought they would.

Margie was home with Allison, so that night I drove myself home in a lot of pain. I parked the car in the garage but could hardly get out of the car. I crawled to the door, and I yelled to Margie that I needed her help. She helped me into the house and to bed.

The next day the team was leaving on a bus for a road trip, and Margie drove me to the team bus. I was in so much pain that I threw up. When the trainer saw my condition, he said, "Go to Northwestern Hospital, right now."

I was hospitalized for four and a half weeks with a broken back and a ruptured disk. Plus, I had no feeling in my right leg.

The doctors recommended acupuncture, physical therapy, and bed rest over surgery. I decided to call Dr. Robert Kerlan, a famous sports orthopedic surgeon in Los Angeles, and got his opinion.

He told me, "Do everything you can to avoid surgery."

CHAPTER 3

Shape the rest of my career

THREE OF MY BULLS TEAMMATES, Jerry Sloan, Tom Boerwinkle and Matty Goukas, came together to visit me one time. But no one from the Chicago Bulls staff or administration came to visit or called me.

One day a stranger showed up in my hospital room and introduced himself as Norm Sonju. At that time, he was the Vice President of Service Master in Chicago. He said he was an avid basketball fan who'd been in a horrible automobile accident, and that his hospitalization had been a lot longer than mine. He encouraged me and prayed with me.

Not long after meeting Norm, I got a call from someone who said, "You won't believe who this is." I said, "Who is it?"

He said, "This is Coach John Wooden. I've heard about you being in the hospital. I've followed your career and I want to encourage you. If there's anything I can do for you when your career's over, just call me at UCLA."

I felt honored that Coach Wooden would take the time to call me and then offer his help. I was encouraged. That call would shape the rest of my career.

I left the hospital and came home, ready to start a new rehab program to come back and play. When I got home that evening, I took a shower and when I got out Margie saw me and exclaimed, "You gotta see your butt!"

When I turned to look in the mirror, there was nothing but skin lying flat on my leg, with no muscle at all.

I wondered if I would be able to play again, but I worked hard for months to get back so I could play again. It started with walking and exercising in a pool. Then I worked with weights, and gradually built up to running. During that time, Margie took good care of me.

After that, I still spent lots of time in bed, staying home with Allison. When Margie would leave the house, we'd put a barrier at the door so Allison couldn't get out. She took her first steps on that bed and that was the beginning of a strong relationship that developed between us.

I played a total of seven minutes in two games in the middle of February. It was obvious I wasn't ready, and so I sat out the rest of the season. I knew I could come back and still play in the NBA, but because I hadn't signed a contract for the year, I was now a free agent.

Three years in a row, Margie and I had driven back to San Diego at the conclusion of the season. Each time, we celebrated her birthday, May 1, at the not-so-stately Pow Wow motel in Tucumcari, New Mexico.

By that time, my back was feeling pretty good, so later that month I drove to Detroit to pick up an Arabian stallion that we had purchased. Because of the long drive to and from Detroit to San Diego, the pain in my back soon returned.

The pain ran down my sciatica nerve, and I developed a "dropped foot," which meant I had no strength in my left foot. I knew I would need an operation, so I got in touch with the top neurosurgeon in town, Dr. David Freeman.

Aside from being a great surgeon, *Sports Illustrated* had recently described him as being the most dominant athlete in the world in his sport, which was badminton.

I had back surgery in June of 1976 and it went really well. I was recovering fast, walking and then jogging on the beach every day. I was also talking to the Lakers about signing a free-agent contract for the upcoming season.

By August I was feeling so good that I decided to try doing some pushups. After the first two or three, my back went into severe spasms, which lasted almost a month. It was so painful that I'd lay on the floor and couldn't get up without Margie's help.

PART 16

SDSU and UCSD

CHAPTER 1

Get on with our lives

My friend Greg Carlson was good friends with Tim Vezie, who had just been named head coach at San Diego State, replacing Dick Davis, who retired.

Tim had just had a back surgery and was rehabbing with the SDSU trainers and therapists. Greg suggested I call Tim to see if SDSU trainers could help get me out of my continuous back spasm.

Tim got me into the training center and in two days I felt some relief. After three days, I was out of the spasm. That spasm had cost me months of recovery. After that, Margie and I had a very serious discussion.

She said, "We need to get on with our lives. I think you need to retire." I said, "I think you're right."

I wrote a short letter to the NBA, notifying the league of my decision to retire.

Because of my involvement with Oakbridge and the horse ranch, I believe I was able to make a better transition than most former NBA players to the next stages of my life.

Within a month after SDSU had started its season, Tim's assistant coach,

Russ Critchfield, decided to move to Northern California. Through the encouragement of Greg Carlson, Tim asked me to fill Critchfield's position.

I negotiated a contract to be part-time because I was working in Ramona on the horse ranch and Oakbridge. As a coach, I was to be involved with planning and evaluating practices with Tim, as well as recruiting, and going on all team trips.

At that same time, Margie got a job as an occupational therapist at the VA Hospital. Every morning, I'd take 2-year-old Allison to Ramona with me to the ranch and Oakbridge.

We'd get back home around 2 pm, so Allison could take a nap with a babysitter, and that's when I'd go to San Diego State to meet with Tim before practice. Margie came home from her job about the time Allison woke up, but I usually didn't get home until 6 or so.

Both of us were working full-time, and we were committed to one of us being with her, except for when she took a nap.

Margie came home from her job about the time Allison woke up, and that's when I'd go to San Diego State to meet with Tim before practice. Of course, we wanted to have at least one of us with her at all times.

I raised Allison to be independent and tough. When she was 2, she was roller-skating as I walked beside her. She caught the skate on some grass and fell on the sidewalk.

She looked at me and said, "That really hurt, Dad. I've got to cry." I said, "Go ahead."

When Allison was 3, Margie and I took her to Yosemite. With us, she hiked up Yosemite Falls, which is about 3,000 vertical feet. Once we reached the top, I put her on my shoulders. Margie had gone ahead to the rock stairs that led to the ledge next to the waterfall.

As I descended the stairs, I tripped, fell forward, and grabbed the railing in front of me that kept us from falling thousands of feet over the edge. Thank God, Margie didn't see it.

I kept Allison on my shoulders, and we hiked back down. That was one of the most harrowing experiences of my life.

—∞∞∞—

Coach Vezie had attended Glendale High and Glendale College four years before I went to both schools. He'd been a star basketball player for both schools and we'd known of each other for some time. When we got together to plan the season, it was evident that we'd get along well together.

However, Tim wanted to run a power offense as Dick Davis had successfully done the year before, but I didn't think that was the best offense for our team. We had two tenacious, competitive guards in Mark Delsman and Dean Decker, and I convinced Tim to let me teach a two-guard offense a little at each practice.

Plus, from last year's team, our star players were Will Connelly and Steve Copp.

Many years later, Mark Delsman became my optometrist, and Steve Copp is now head of orthopedics at Scripps Clinic, and became my orthopedic surgeon.

Going into our first league game at Cal State Fullerton, we were 3–11 running the power offense. At halftime, we were down double digits. I told Tim that this would be a good time to put in the two-guard offense and let the guards start full-court pressing. We started Joel Kramer at center instead of Will Connelly.

We had nothing to lose, and we won by double digits. We used the two-guard offense the rest of the season and won our league.

The following year, we recruited well. One of the players Tim and I had a home visit with was Tony Gwynn, a point guard who came to SDSU on a basketball scholarship.

Later, of course, he became a Hall of Fame baseball superstar with the San Diego Padres.

Mike Dodd was also one of the standout players on those teams. I had the privilege of baptizing Mike in a friend's hot tub after he expressed his faith in Jesus. He would later become an Olympic Gold medalist in beach volleyball.

CHAPTER 2

He said it was a miracle

IN APRIL 1979, Margie was pregnant with our son, Jeff.

She had extremely high blood pressure during her pregnancy and had to be monitored closely. She was around seven-and-a-half months pregnant when she was diagnosed with pre-eclampsia.

Her doctors hospitalized her and gave her a drug that put her into false labor to test what might happen next. The doctor said I could go home.

As soon as I got home, the doctor called and said that it was no longer a false labor and that I needed to get back to the hospital. When I arrived, the doctor said they wanted to delay labor because her blood pressure was so high.

The doctor asked if I had any idea of how to get her blood pressure down. Immediately, I recalled playing the game of "Master Mind" many times in the car with her, without using the board. It required deep concentration.

Margie was awake, but in deep trouble. I'm not sure she knew how much trouble she was in, but they decided they couldn't deliver the baby yet. I said, "Margie, let's play Master Mind." She said OK. We started playing and her blood pressure started coming down.

As soon as it got low enough, they took her into the delivery room right away. Within minutes I was holding my son, a three-pound, 11-ounce baby. I was tremendously relieved and filled with joy as I looked at him. I was also thankful that I had been trained to remain calm under stressful situations.

They placed Jeff into an incubator and said we could take him home when he was at a healthy weight.

I had learned throughout my life not to pump myself up emotionally. From the time I was a boy working in a gas station with my dad until his death, then on to Harlem and the NBA, I trained myself to rein in my emotions.

Rudy La Russo had taught me that I would wear myself out if I got too emotional, and that I needed to be level-headed throughout a game.

Later, when I met with Coach John Wooden, he reinforced the idea of raising the level of intensity as the situation requires. He told me that the great athletes learn to control their intensity while staying focused and relaxed. I had a measure of that.

I didn't realize the gravity of the situation until the doctor said, "We were close to losing them both, before you came." He said it was a miracle that I had thought about playing a game to bring her blood pressure down.

Jeff was in intensive care for five days. When we brought him home to La Jolla, I took him down to the shore, and, as I had done with Allison, I dedicated him to God.

When Jeff was about a year and a half, he was having ear aches like crazy. Margie took him to the doctor and they put tubes into his ears. He did well for a time, and then his ear aches returned.

The doctor said the infection was so bad that he couldn't even see the tubes. He said we had to get rid of the infection before he could take the tubes out. He recommended that we see our pediatrician, and we made an appointment to see him the next day.

Jeff was suffering greatly that night, and we brought him in and laid him between us in our bed. I prayed, "Lord, I don't know how to pray for Jeff, but he's your child. Please heal him."

We prayed that simple prayer as we laid hands on him. The next day the doctor looked into his ears and there was no infection and no tubes. The doctor said, "There's nothing wrong with him."

He hasn't had a problem with his ears since.

CHAPTER 3

The why of everything

OUR NEIGHBOR IN LA JOLLA, Ted Forbes, and I played a lot of beach volleyball together. He and another administrator at UCSD approached me with an offer to become the school's head basketball coach.

I put in an application and was hired.

Once Margie and I made the decision that coaching would be my career, I made an appointment to see Coach Wooden at his office at Pauley Pavilion on the UCLA campus. I spent three hours with him discussing coaching philosophy.

He drilled into me the importance of always teaching the why of everything. He said that if the players understand what you teach and agree with it, then it's just a matter of effort and technique.

I've used that philosophy in all areas of my life.

Another important thing Coach Wooden told me was not to imitate another coach's style. You know who you are, and you coach out of that understanding. That comment gave me freedom.

We talked about how to organize practices, and how to keep all of your players engaged throughout the practice. He was a stickler for being on time to practices and all meetings. If you were late, there were consequences.

Later that afternoon, I went to Palos Verdes, where I spent three hours with Coach Pete Newell, who had been the general manager when I played with the San Diego Rockets.

He was also a tremendous coach and won an NCAA Basketball Championship at Cal Berkley. He mentored many coaches, including Bobby Knight. We discussed many of the same things Coach Wooden and I had talked about, but from Newell's perspective, as he also talked about the concept of why.

The conclusion I reached from my time with Coach Wooden and Coach Newell was that high achievement comes from vision, planning, assessment of talent, flexibility to adapt to various circumstances, commitment, focus and discipline.

As I got better and better at understanding the why of everything, I began seeing that's what the Bible taught.

When I look at Paul's writing in the New Testament, I see how he structures his letters, with teaching the why first, then explaining the practical application of how we are to live.

My life verse for the why of life is Romans 11: 36.

For from Him, and through Him and to Him are all things.

To Him be glory forever.

Amen.

CHAPTER 4

Changing the culture

ONE OF MARGIE'S FRIENDS from the VA Hospital in La Jolla was a psychiatrist named David Sunde. We became good friends as he loved basketball and loved horses. He grew up on a horse farm in Michigan, where he had trained horses before going to medical school.

He also had a faith in Jesus, and we shared many hours of discussing theology, horse training, and sports psychology.

Because it was my first time as a head coach, I invited him to attend one of my practices and evaluate the way I coached. He taught me how to better present myself as a leader. He told me to keep my hands out of my pockets, look at the players, and have the players look at me.

He encouraged me to speak loudly enough so all the players could hear what I was saying. He suggested that I shouldn't sit down during practices, unless the entire team was also sitting.

Most coaches will give a direction and tack on the word, "Okay?" Sunde suggested that I should avoid using "okay" because that turns a direction into a question, as if asking for the player's approval.

When I took over as head coach in 1980, UCSD had only achieved a few winning seasons since the program's inception in 1965. I knew I had to change the culture. That meant I needed players who knew how to play hard, were teachable, and followed my instructions.

I assessed the whole situation and what was behind all those losing seasons.

One reason was the university's policy of not giving athletic scholarships. UCSD belonged to the NAIA (National Association of Intercollegiate Athletics), which meant they competed against schools that *did* give scholarships and were far better.

Every season, schools looked forward to scheduling us because it was almost always an automatic win for them. So, I started to schedule those kinds of wins for our team. Most of all, I wanted our team to learn what it was like to win, especially early in the season.

I'm a firm believer that spectator sports are all about entertainment. What's most needed is a team that plays hard, is exciting, and wins, something I knew we could attain.

At that time, however, attendance for UCSD's home games numbered only about 50 fans. My challenge was, how could I get more people to attend our games?

Besides winning, I knew we needed to create excitement about the program. First, I reached out to the campus student leaders and asked them what needed to be done to create an entertaining atmosphere. Then I helped organize a cheerleading squad, and I encouraged them to be creative with their cheers and perform a themed halftime program.

I went to their practices to check on their progress, and interacted with student life leaders to come up with ways to create events and bring more students to our games.

That led to Spirit Night, a spirit competition between each of the UCSD colleges. Winning the competition required combined scores for best theme, best spirit, and best floats.

From the very first Spirit Night, the gym was packed. Of course, I had scheduled a sure win for that night. I'm pleased to say that Spirit Night continues to this day.

My good friend, Jeff Reinke, who was a high-level beach volleyball player, became my first assistant coach. We had met through my friends, Skip and Tracey Stratton, with whom I also played beach volleyball.

Jeff had played basketball at Pasadena High for George Terzian before attending USC on a basketball scholarship. He was also a pitcher for the USC baseball team that won three national championships.

Drafted by the Detroit Tigers, he eventually became the overseer of Oakbridge's sports camps.

We bonded primarily because of our shared faith in God, and our love and experience with basketball, baseball and beach volleyball. We started playing volleyball together almost immediately with some mutual friends, including Bob Marlowe and Pat McDougall, who had been a volleyball star at San Diego State.

Judy Sweet served as UCSD's athletic director during my three years there. She later became president of the NCAA and was inducted to the San Diego Sports Hall of Champions. We were both strong personalities, and I found her to be a very capable professional and a good listener.

Judy ran a tight ship because her resources were extremely limited. As a result, I had to be creative to help fund the basketball program.

One of the ways was scheduling games with D-1 programs that guaranteed money for us to come play them. Fresno State was on the schedule that first year and gave us a big financial guarantee.

They beat us by 58 points, but we were now in better financial shape.

We started the season with 15 players and ended with eight. The players who left either quit, or I asked them to leave.

At the end of that season, a young man named Tom Marshall came into my office and told me, "I'm interested in being your assistant coach. I want to learn from you, and I'll do whatever you want me to do, and you don't have to pay me."

He was a successful high school basketball coach in the area, and I hired him on the spot.

Tom would eventually be a Ring of Honor recipient for his 11-year coaching career at UCSD.

CHAPTER 5

Our prayers were answered

ONE EVENING, I WAS IN A UCSD athletic department staff meeting when Margie called and told me, "Jeff's had an accident. You need to come to the hospital."

He was only 18 months old and had tripped while holding a toothbrush. Margie thought he had poked his eye out. I raced to the hospital and the doctor said he couldn't do anything yet because there was so much blood and swelling.

The doctor thought he might lose sight in that eye, and we wouldn't know until the following day. Jeff spent the night in the hospital in great pain. They gave him a shot so he could sleep, but he reacted the opposite way and was wide awake and still in great pain.

Margie and I held him tightly the entire night.

I called Don Williams, who had then moved with his wife, Tap, to San Diego. I asked him to come to the hospital and pray for Jeff. When Don arrived at the hospital, we all laid hands on Jeff and prayed for healing. In the morning, the doctor told us that there was no damage to the eye itself.

The eyelid required 72 stitches, and the only permanent damage was in the function of the tear duct.

Our prayers were answered.

We realized again that the Lord had his hand on Jeff, who loves God and the scriptures. He recently spent three years teaching Bible, while his wife taught English literature in a high school in Quito, Ecuador. He has received notes from his students telling him that they appreciated him teaching them how to think.

CHAPTER 6

A Chance to Win

MY SECOND YEAR AT UCSD, we were a young team, competing in the league tournament playoff game with the top D-3 team in the nation, Biola University. The head coach, Dave Holmquist, was a brilliant coach and a gracious person.

This was the beginning of a wonderful rivalry that would last over 20 years while I coached at different colleges. This time, Biola had beaten us by 48 points just two weeks before. They were a ridiculously good team, almost D-1 caliber. We were the No. 8 seed playing the No. 1 seed, on their home court in Los Angeles.

I figured the only way we could win was to stall, which was legal at the time. The score at halftime was 18–10, Biola. At halftime, I told the players that we were going to shorten the game.

The rule at that time was that the ball had to be advanced every few seconds over a short black line on the sideline. So, using a stalling tactic, I had two players pass the ball over that line in front of our bench for 10 straight minutes, and thus "shorten" the game.

The crowd was going crazy, mocking me by passing their tennis shoes back and forth as if they were basketballs. It was perfect. We were only down by about 15 or 16 points with about four minutes to go when they inserted a 7-6 player who didn't play much.

When they did, I called a time-out and told my players that we had a chance to win this game. Then I told them to foul the 7-6 player whenever Biola got possession of the ball.

After he went to the free-throw line and missed all his shots, Coach Holmquist called time out and had him take the ball out of bounds, hoping we wouldn't foul him again.

I asked the referee if we could foul the player while he was out of bounds, and he said we could. So, I told my team to foul him, even if he was out of bounds. The rules have changed since. He shot 16 free throws and made only one before he was subbed out.

They were a vastly superior team to ours, but we ended up losing by only 12 points.

When Coach Holmquist and I were shaking hands, he said, "That was one of the best coaching jobs I've ever seen."

After talking with the team, I came back onto the court where a lot of students and fans were still milling around. A few of them were telling me how awful I was.

One man in particular, dressed in a suit and tie, was so aggressive with me that the father of one of my players had to step between us. He was yelling at me, calling me the worst sportsman he had ever seen.

It was a Thursday night when we drove home from the game around midnight. I left home and drove an hour to the ranch, because we had two of our mares, who were sisters, ready to deliver foals. I drove out there for the night to monitor them. I had a video system set up in the stalls to check on the mares.

That weekend, Oakbridge had rented the facility for a men's retreat from a church in Fullerton. On Saturday morning I joined the group for breakfast, and they asked me to share my testimony of my faith in Jesus. In my sharing, I spoke about the game at Biola.

After speaking, we left the dining area. A small group of men were chuckling as I approached them. I asked them what was so funny, and they said they heard all about the game from their speaker, a Biola professor who had been there.

I asked where he was, and they said he was still in the dining room waiting until you're gone.

Just then he came out and it turned out that he was the same man who had been in my face after the game. I told him we needed to talk. We did, and I explained to him about competition and playing within the rules and how a coach has to do whatever he can to help his team win.

His response was, "If I had known you were a Christian, I wouldn't have acted that way."

Really?

CHAPTER 7

He asked me about my faith

ONE OF THE HIGHLIGHTS of my coaching career was when I scheduled Loyola Marymount, a D-1 school, to play on their home court.

The reason for the game was for us to have the experience of playing against better teams and get the guarantee to augment our budget. Ed Goorjian, the coach who had grabbed me out of line to play basketball in high school, was the head coach there.

Goorjian's son, Greg, was the star of their team and a tremendous scorer.

Although it was a long shot, I really believed we had a chance to win. I had put together a "match-up zone defense" that matches up to different types of offenses and adjusts to the different types of players.

We entered the game with a solid plan that would exploit their weaknesses and make it difficult for their top scorers to score. We ended up winning.

It might have been the first time a team that didn't use scholarships had beaten a D-1 team in the history of California. It was an especially rewarding win for my point guard, Bobby Goodman, who had transferred from Loyola Marymount to UCSD.

After the season, I got a call from legendary coach Jerry Tarkanian. He said he had a player that would be a good fit for UCSD and asked me if I'd be interested in having him join my team.

The University of San Francisco had shut down its basketball program and two of its best players had transferred to UNLV to play with Coach Tarkanian.

He didn't have enough room on the roster for Steve Flint, who was a very good student, and a dedicated, hard-playing player. I told Coach Tarkanian, yes, for sure I could use him on our team.

When Steve began attending UCSD, he came into my office and said he wanted to be a pro basketball player and asked if I could help him attain that goal.

I told him, "See that door? All you have to do is knock on it and I'll come work with you."

So, every time he knocked on that door, we went to the court and worked together on improving his game. Tom Marshall, who wanted to learn everything from me, was there to learn also. Steve ended up playing professionally overseas for a number of years.

In my third year at UCSD in the 1982–'83 season, I was recruiting a player from Moorpark Community College, coached by Al Nordquist. I was on the phone with Al, talking about his player, when he asked me about my faith in Jesus. He had heard that I was a believer.

After a bit of discussion, he asked if I was interested in going to the NCAA Final Four in Albuquerque, New Mexico with his good friend, George Terzian. I had known George from his days of coaching high school ball in Pasadena, and he was now Pasadena Community College's head coach.

When Al asked me, I immediately replied, "I'd love to."

That first trip forged a relationship with these men and changed the direction of my life. I would attend the Final Four with Al and George for the next 22 years and it was always deeply impactful.

While we were in New Mexico that first year, George and Al introduced me to Ken Hayes, who had just been fired from Oral Roberts University (ORU).

When we met with Ken in our room, he told us the circumstances of his firing. After ORU lost to its cross-town rival, the University of Tulsa, his higher-ups were very angry and fired him immediately after the game. We were able to pray with Ken and encourage him.

Little did I know that the next season I would be coaching at ORU.

PART 17

Oral Roberts

CHAPTER 1

It was all about me

DURING MY FIVE YEARS OF COACHING at SDSU and UCSD, the first phase of Oakbridge was built. We had basketball camps and Stan Smith tennis camps and we also rented the camp out for retreats.

During that time, Margie and I decided to incorporate our horse breeding and showing operation as Ballena Valley Arabians. We moved the ranch from Ramona to a ten-acre parcel in Olivenhain.

There, I started building the ranch again from nothing, and became an elder at Mt. Soledad Presbyterian Church, pastored by Don Williams.

Meanwhile, our son Jeff was born and our daughter Allison started school.

Toward the end of those five years, I was a physical and emotional wreck. The stress and pressure of all I was doing was overwhelming. The stress of the time I spent coaching, combined with managing Oakbridge and the day-to-day running of our Arabian horse ranch left little time for my family.

Amid all that were the difficult financial stresses Margie and I were experiencing.

Along the way, I had lost my first love, Jesus, and it was now all about me. I knew I had to do something. Needing repentance, I went to Oakbridge and climbed onto some big rocks that overlook the camp.

Weeping, I cried out to the Lord, "I'm done. I'm giving all of this to you." I immediately resigned from being the overseer and president of the board of Oakbridge.

Within a week or two of my resignation from Oakbridge, I got a call from Pat Harrison, whose family I had lived with when I was with the Rockets. Pat was assistant baseball coach at ORU at that time, which was the spring of my third season at UCSD.

Pat asked if I could meet with him and Larry Cochell, ORU's baseball coach and newly appointed athletic director. They were going to be in Pomona, California for a baseball tournament and asked me to meet them there.

As it turned out, Margie and I were going to be in Pomona for an Arabian horse show at the same time.

Was that a coincidence?

After ORU fired Ken Hayes, whom I had met with at the Final Four weeks earlier, Larry had to promote Ken's assistant, Dick Acres, to the head coaching position. Dick had been a successful basketball coach for Carson High School prior to coming to ORU.

The athletic department, along with Oral Roberts himself, who was deeply involved in the basketball team, realized that Dick didn't have enough experience to be named head coach.

They wanted me to be Dick's assistant coach because of my college experience and recruiting abilities. Dick's sons were the best players on the team, and the feeling was that if Dick was not hired as head coach, his boys would transfer.

I told him that I thought hiring him would be a huge mistake, and that I was not interested in being his assistant. Larry asked me as a favor to reconsider and come visit ORU. I agreed and one week later I was in Tulsa.

The university flew me out and "wined" and dined me, of course without the wine, in keeping with ORU's no-alcohol policy. It was an impressive campus and basketball facility. It was evident they really wanted me.

When Larry asked again if I would take the job, I told him I didn't think so. He arranged to fly back with me to Chicago, on my way back to San Diego.

On the plane, he asked, "What would it take for you to become our assistant coach?" I threw out a ridiculous salary number that was higher than many D-1 head coaches made at that time. He looked over at me and said, "Done!"

I was shocked, and then said, "Okay."

In the midst of all that turmoil, God provided.

CHAPTER 2

What was God up to now?

I HAD TO CONTINUALLY PRAY and seek God's wisdom through the scriptures. I had just gone through an emotional, internal upheaval with Oakbridge and the moving of the ranch.

Now I knew there would be challenges as an assistant coach at ORU. Usually, college coaches hire their own assistants. So, I knew it was going to be tough being an assistant coach to a head coach who didn't hire me.

I knew I was there not for myself, but to serve and glorify God. I was also there to serve the head coach, the players and the university. I often had to remind myself why I was there.

After I was hired, Jeff Reinke was hired as the athletic chaplain. He was attending Gordon-Conwell Seminary near Boston, originally to get his master's degree in Divinity and to help plant a church with Bill Randall, the former worship leader at Mt. Soledad Presbyterian.

Jeff had spent one year there, when Larry Cochell called to offer him the position. Now we were together at Oral Roberts.

What was God up to now?

As we had done when I was in the NBA, Margie and our children stayed in San Diego until I rented a house for us. An Arabian horse breeder in Jenks, a suburb of Tulsa, offered to sell us a 15-acre horse ranch just down the road from him.

It was only minutes from ORU and it had pecan and oak trees on the property, pasture fencing, a six-horse barn and a three-bedroom house. It was perfect for us. We moved our 15 horses and all the equipment needed for the ranch.

One of the other assistant coaches, Dolph Carroll, and I drove my truck to Olivenhain to pick up the last of our horses and all of the equipment, including a Massy Ferguson skip loader tractor. I rented the largest U-Haul truck and bought a used flatbed trailer to transport the tractor.

With me driving the U-Haul and Dolph driving the truck with the two horses in the horse trailer, we took off for Tulsa.

By the time we reached Tucson, Arizona, the U-Haul had broken down six times, so we decided to stop at a large U-Haul facility. They gave us another truck and helped us unload and re-load the truck and tractor, which the owner of the facility offered to buy.

In the very frustrated mood I was in, I said yes and tossed out a figure that was three times the amount I had paid for it. To my surprise, he agreed. We spent the night in Tucson and took off the next morning with a much lighter load.

When we got to New Mexico, I stopped and called Margie.

She asked where I was, and I told her we wouldn't be home until the next day because of all of our delays. She was relieved and said that it was raining so hard in Tulsa that a hundred-year flood was hitting the area.

She said our ranch was all but underwater to the second rail of our fencing and nearly to our front door. Things were so bad that there were places where cars were stacked on top of each other.

The next morning, we kept driving and arrived within a day. The storm had blown through.

CHAPTER 3

A major teaching point in my life

WE WERE STILL RECRUITING in late spring when George Terzian called me to say he had a player he thought would be good for us.

His name was Charles Dorsey, a tremendous guard who ended up starting for us for two years. He set a record for field-goal percentage in a game at ORU by hitting 11-for-11 against Butler University.

Charles met his wife at ORU and is now the pastor of a church in the Los Angeles area.

Meanwhile, there was a lot of controversy around Oral Roberts himself, and I had heard a lot of criticism of him. It appeared to me that he had taken ownership of the ministry God had given him.

One day, I told Pat Harrison, "I know some of what he's going through and why it happened, because it had happened to me at Oakbridge."

That was a major teaching point in my life, and so I never condemned Oral. I told the Lord, "If you put me in a situation like that again, I won't ever take ownership again. It's all about you Lord and your glory."

That sentiment would be tested.

At the beginning, coaching with Dick Acres was like walking a tightrope. I wanted to help him be the best coach he could be, and the basketball program to be the best it could be. That's what an assistant coach does.

I needed to be a teacher and coach not only to the players, but to our inexperienced coaching staff, too. Dick and the staff handled the situation very well.

I helped organize the practices and oversaw recruiting. One of the things Coach Wooden taught me was to keep players moving, not to let them stand around during practice. He told me to keep practices organized so the players go from here to there and are running and moving the entire time.

Oral attended one of the practices, and had just come out of the rain wearing his raincoat and a cool fedora hat. "That's a great hat," I said.

He replied, "You really think so? I've lost this hat three times while traveling around the world, and I always got it back. It means a lot to me."

Then he took it off and gave it to me. This was acting out his ministry foundation and belief in "seed faith." I was amazed and grateful to receive a gift that meant a lot to him.

Although we had numerous difficulties to overcome, we managed to have a really successful season, winning our league and going to the NCAA playoffs.

But after I got fired a year or so later, Margie threw that hat away.

CHAPTER 4

'I can't do the work"

THE NEXT SEASON, I was recruiting Willie Irons, the second-ranked prospect in the state of Oklahoma.

Willie was a 17-year-old, left-handed African American. In his senior year at Tulsa High, I attended his practices and games and developed a strong relationship with him. He had a challenging childhood, living in other teammates' homes all through high school.

I liked him a lot. He was driven, and wanted to go to college, something nobody in his family had ever done. He committed to playing basketball at ORU and was very excited to start classes. After about a month of school, one of his teachers called me and said he had skipped many of his classes.

I immediately went to his dorm and knocked on his door.

There was no answer, but I kept knocking and said, "Willie, I know you're in there. This is Coach Block." He got up from his bed, came to the door and let me in. I sat down with him and asked what was going on.

He said, "Coach, I can't do the work, I can't keep up and I don't understand what they're saying." I asked him if he still wanted to earn a college education. He said he did and I said, "Okay, let me work on this."

Oral Roberts University is strong academically and at that time had an entire student diagnostic center. I told them Willie needed to be tested academically. He willingly took the tests that revealed he had a decent IQ, but an informational base of zero, and was reading at a third-grade level.

With no informational base, he had no experience to draw on.

We decided to have him flunk all his classes so that we could get him a full-time tutor. The tutor started teaching him to read out of comic books. She took him to museums and other places of interest around Tulsa, working on his informational base.

He worked hard and by semester's end he was up to a 10th grade reading level and his informational base had improved. He started taking basic classes and he was doing well. By the school year's end, he was reading at a 12th grade level.

From then on, he passed all his classes. He worked hard and the university really worked with him. Through Willie, the university discovered there were quite a few students in the same situation as he was, so they created a few reading classes for them.

Also, they created an African American history class, which Willie enjoyed. Since he had flunked his classes the first semester, he had to go to full-time summer school to be eligible to play the following year, which he did willingly.

At Christmas time, I asked Willie if he knew of a poor family who needed food for Christmas dinner. He said he knew of a single mother and her children who were in need.

All of the black players and I chipped in to buy groceries for this family. When we showed up on her doorstep with bags of groceries, she shed tears of joy and gratitude. The players were also moved and thankful.

There was a chapel session scheduled where some of the school's athletes were going to lead everything from worship, giving testimonies and presenting the message. Jeff Reinke put the whole thing together, including a band where I played my acoustic guitar.

It was so exciting to be up on stage, helping lead the worship with other athletes and coaches. The entire place was filled with the Spirit of God. At the end of the chapel, a student yelled out from the top of the balcony, "God is really pleased with what just happened."

We all replied, "Amen."

CHAPTER 5

A slam dunk

I started recruiting a 6-10 highly regarded player in northern Iowa named Steve Phyfe. After first seeing him play, I knew he would be perfect for our program, so I went after him.

Every weekend for eight weeks, I flew from Tulsa to Des Moines, Iowa, driving three hours, once through a blizzard, to watch him play. The gym was packed, so every night I had to arrive early. The family saved me a seat in front of them, even though, according to the NCAA rules, I was not supposed to talk with them.

Steve signed with ORU, but only played one year before transferring to Northern Iowa University because the entire coaching staff, including me, was fired. Not surprisingly, he went on to have a successful college basketball career.

Not long ago our family was discussing our experience in Tulsa and Allison mentioned that it was hard for them because I was gone every weekend, constantly recruiting and traveling all over the country.

It was a tough time for all of us.

Through one of my connections from my Harlem experience, a coach from the Bronx connected me with one of his players. He was a 6-10 African American player named Teviin Binns, who was a sophomore with the highly prominent basketball team at Midland Junior College in Texas. I got in touch with him and his coach.

It was early in the year, and we were one of the first colleges to recruit him. I first went to see him play at his first home game. I saw a well-dressed man sitting alone in the stands at midcourt. I went and sat next to him and discovered that he owned a highly successful oil company.

Interestingly, he was Teviin's "sponsor," which meant that he helped him financially. As we discussed our program and my career, we connected. He said that whenever I came to town, he would pick me up from the airport, and that I could use his Mercedes and stay in his guest house.

I made many trips to Texas to watch Teviin play. When he played an away game, I would fly to Midland and drive to the game with my new best friend.

Later, North Carolina State started recruiting him. When it came time for a commitment and then signing of a letter of intent, Teviin committed to play for ORU. His decision was supported not only by his coach in the Bronx, but also by his dad and his "sponsor."

We thought this was a slam-dunk.

When it came to sign Teviin, I went to Los Angeles to try and sign another player while our other assistant coach went to sign Teviin.

I got a call from Dolph saying that Teviin was being "hot boxed" by the assistant coach from NC State and the head coach of Midland. This meant that they had isolated him. When Dolph couldn't get to Teviin, I told him I'd call his dad and find out what was going on.

When I talked to his dad, he told me there was nothing he could do. The reality was that they were going to give both Teviin and his father an under-the-table payment, plus a car. As a result, Teviin signed with NC State.

I was disappointed and angry.

A little later, ORU's golf coach told me how he was flying to North Carolina and was seated next to NC State's assistant coach. He asked the coach if he had signed any new players, and the assistant coach replied that he had signed Teviin Binns, but that he wouldn't play much.

Then he said that NC State would never be out-recruited by Oral Roberts University.

I had my first taste of corruption as a D-1 coach.

CHAPTER 6

Trust Jesus for my future

WHEN DICK ACRES WAS COACHING at Carson High in California, he was also a referee. For some reason, he really got after the referees during games. That was especially so when calls were made against or not made for his two sons.

ORU's home arena, the Mabee Center, had a raised floor that required walking up two steps. Coach Acres would go up those stairs and start yelling and gesturing at the referees. Because of the elevation of the raised floor the spotlight was on him.

Referees are only human, and they don't like to be embarrassed. If there was a doubt on a call, the call would go against Coach Acres' sons. As assistant coaches, we really tried to calm him, telling him it was hurting the team *and* his sons.

Toward the end of the season, athletic director Larry Cochell told Coach Acres that Oral Roberts didn't care for his in-game behavior. Before one game, we came out on the floor and we were shocked to see Oral seated next to where Dick Acres always sat.

I always sat next to Dick, so he was between Oral and me.

Oral hadn't said a word the entire game until Dick got up and started yelling at the referees. Oral got off his chair, stepped up on the first stair, grabbed Dick's coattails, pulled him down into his seat and said, "Mister, sit down. You'll not embarrass my ministry anymore."

His ministry?

The local news station was doing highlights of the game and had recorded the whole event. Guess what played on the nightly news? The commentator asked, "Is Dick Acres long for this job?"

Almost immediately after the season, Dick was fired. I was then asked to apply for the head coaching position, which I did.

Things were going well for me in terms of interviews when it came down to two finalists: me and Ken Trickey, a former head coach who in 1974 took ORU to the Elite Eight in the NCAA Tournament, a tremendous achievement for a small school.

A few days later, however, he'd been picked up for drunk driving and was subsequently fired. Still, after all these years, they were now reconsidering him for head coach.

I was being interviewed by the members of ORU's athletic board, chaired by my friend Dr. Jim Winslow. Rosey Grier, the pro football Hall of Famer, was there as a board member. He was a great guy and we knew each other pretty well.

The meeting was going smoothly until I was asked a question by Richard Roberts, Oral's son. "Do you speak in tongues?" he asked. I hesitated and then said, "No, Richard, God hasn't gifted me with that yet."

He leaned forward and said, "Don't you know this ministry is founded on that principal!" The meeting ended abruptly, soon after that comment.

A few nights later I got a call around 11 pm from Dr. Jim Winslow. He asked if I could come to the City of Faith Hospital, right then. That's the hospital Oral's ministry had personally financed, and Jim was the head of the facility. I wondered why they wanted to talk to me so late.

When I arrived, I was very surprised to see that along with Jim and Richard Roberts, Ken Trickey was there.

Their opening statement to me was that they felt that I would be good as a head coach for the long term, and that Ken would be good for the short term. They wanted to know if I would agree to be Ken's assistant. The discussion centered around Ken making a case for himself to Richard and Jim.

I didn't say three sentences in an hour.

When the meeting ended, Jim asked me to come into his office. He said, "You didn't say much in the meeting." He asked me what I thought, and I told him there was no way I could work with Ken Trickey, especially because of the way he had expressed himself in the previous meeting.

A few days later, Oral came into my office, sat down and wanted to talk, as he sometimes did. The focus of his words was that I really needed to trust Jesus for my future. The next day, ORU made the surprise announcement that the school had hired former Kansas head coach Ted Owens as its new head coach.

I was retained as an assistant coach.

Soon after Ted was hired, he and I traveled to Nigeria together to see Osaro Onaiwu, a 6–9 raw talent who ended up attending ORU. He was too raw a talent for Ted Owens, but I saw his potential.

Later, in Coach Owen's office, he said, "The problem with you, Block, is that you believe you can make that chair into a player."

I replied, "If that chair has a heart, I *will* make it into a player."

I took his words as a compliment.

After this, Ted surprised the staff by saying he was going to interview for another assistant coach, who was coming in the next day. This coach was known for his recruiting prowess, and Dolph and I were asked by Ted to take part in the interview.

After the coach left, Ted asked us our opinion of him. Dolph Carroll and I immediately agreed that he shouldn't hire this coach. However, he was still hired.

That summer I was scheduled to be in Los Angeles on recruiting trips. I decided that my family and I would drive there with the intent of being there around a month. After about three weeks, I got a call from Ted Owens.

The first thing he said was, "Just listen to me. I want you to drive back immediately and not use the university credit card." I knew I was being fired, but I just said, "All right, I'll leave right away."

When I arrived home, I went to see athletic director Larry Cochell, who told me that while he was recruiting, Ted had talked to Oral about firing me. Turns out there was a written list of grievances against me, provided by the newly-hired assistant coach.

Based upon those alleged grievances, Oral had agreed to have me fired. Larry gave me the list and after going over each one, I became angry because none of them were true. I asked Larry to call board president Jim Winslow and set up a meeting immediately. Larry and I went to meet with him, so I could explain the truth.

When we met, I went through the list one by one. About halfway through, I could see that Jim was becoming agitated. He said he was going to get me reinstated, and I said, "No, you're not. There's no way I can continue working here."

I didn't say much more.

Now what?

PART 18

Gordon College

CHAPTER 1

'I don't want to go East'

I WASN'T SURE WHAT I WANTED to do next, but a few days later I got a call from our close friends, Bob and Kay Goshen, who were extremely successful in Amway. At their urging, I decided to become an Amway distributor under the Goshen's sponsorship.

I went through all the training, but after a few months I realized it simply wasn't for me because I didn't like sales. After that, I met a guy who was into financial planning. Somehow, he talked me into getting my Series 7 license to sell insurance products and give financial advice.

I soon realized that wasn't for me either. In sales you have to do "the ask." I hated "the ask." I wanted to get back to coaching basketball. I could certainly do the ask when recruiting players.

Meanwhile, it was spring, time for the NCAA Final Four in Dallas. The previous year, I had attended the Final Four with my friends, Al Nordquist and George Terzian.

This year Paul Westphal was also planning to go to the Final Four. He was looking for a coaching job, as was I, so we decided to travel to Dallas and share a room in the same hotel where the National Association of Basketball Coaches (NABC) was headquartered.

The day before the Final Four games began, Al, George and I were having lunch in the hotel lobby. My friend, Chet Kammerer, who was coaching basketball for Westmont College, approached us.

He asked me if I'd be interested in talking to a representative from Gordon College about the position of athletic director and basketball coach. I asked him where Gordon was and he said it was in the Boston area, in the town of Wenham. I said, "I don't want to go East, I want to go West."

He said, "Do me a favor and just meet with their representative."

I agreed, and walked over to meet with Dave Macmillan, the vice president of development at Gordon College. He informed me that Gordon was a sister school of Westmont College and that its school's leaders were committed to improving the athletic program, especially in basketball.

After some discussion, I politely said that I wasn't interested.

I didn't have tickets to the NCAA games and was going to watch them on a big screen TV in the hotel's large convention room. I came down the escalator to order some food at the hotel deli.

As I stood in line, Dave Macmillan came over to ask if he could sit with me as I watched the Final Four, and I said, "Sure."

Later, he told me he had been talking to his wife on a pay phone, saying that he had struck out and was coming home. Just as he said that to her, he saw me coming down the escalator and told his wife, "I've got to go," and hung up.

We sat together, barely watching the games. Instead, we discussed our faith and the college's philosophy of athletics, which impressed me. By the end of our conversation, I told him that I had really enjoyed our time together, but that I still wasn't interested in going to Gordon College.

As we said our goodbyes, he gave me his business card.

The final game was on Monday, but I decided to fly back to Tulsa on Sunday to be with my family. I watched the championship game at home with Jeff Reinke.

At halftime, Jeff asked me how it went in Dallas. I told him that Dave Macmillan asked me if I was interested in being athletic director and basketball coach at Gordon College. Jeff was amazed, since he was planning to return to the Gordon College area to assist with a church that he had helped start.

Jeff had even applied for a job at Gordon and thought it would be good if we could go there together. He also mentioned that there was a lot of demonic activity in that area, as the campus is close to Salem, site of infamous Salem Witch Trials.

Amazing. What was God up to now?

CHAPTER 2

A big logistical problem

I GOT OUT DAVE MACMILLAN'S CARD and called him immediately.

When I asked Dave if he was still interested in talking to me about the position at Gordon, I sensed that he just about jumped through the phone. He asked if I could visit the campus that week. I flew there, toured the area and met with the Gordon College president, Dick Gross.

He and I connected immediately.

I'd been in Oklahoma for several years, seeing nothing but flat terrain. Now, being in New England amid all those large and very old trees made me feel so claustrophobic that I asked the driver to take me to the coast, only a couple of miles from the Gordon campus.

Margie and I agreed that I would take the position, so I became athletic director and head basketball coach at Gordon College. This created a big logistics problem for us because we had to move our 15 horses and a ranch full of equipment from Jenks, Oklahoma.

The cost of boarding the horses alone would be more than my salary.

I decided to lease out some of our mares, and one of them was going to Louisville, Kentucky. I asked Jeff Reinke, who was still seeking a job in the Gordon College area, if he'd like to go to Louisville with me to deliver the mare. He said he had nothing else to do, so he agreed to come along.

On that drive I got a phone call from Margie, who told me that Gordon needed a women's volleyball coach. Jeff and I were discussing who might be good when I said, "What about you?"

He had played a lot of volleyball, but had never coached it. I convinced him that he could do the job. Right there, driving in my pickup truck, I conducted the interview and hired him to be women's volleyball coach and our baseball coach.

Before we had moved, Dick Gross asked me to attend a charity golf tournament with him in Rhode Island. That was the first of many golf outings we had together. As we were driving back to Gordon, he asked if I had found a place for our family and our horses.

I said we hadn't found anything yet, and that finding something to meet our needs seemed almost impossible.

He thought there might be an opportunity on an estate owned by Mrs. Phillips, a wealthy, eccentric woman who helped support Gordon College. Her family had founded Phillips Academy and Phillips Exeter Academy.

The next day we met with Mrs. Phillips in Salem at one of her two mansions. She owned a 100-acre estate with a 10,000 square foot house, and three other smaller residences that she rented out.

The estate was located in the North Shore of Massachusetts, part of one of the most expensive regions in the country, the town of Topsfield, near Boxford.

Mrs. Phillips said that the family living in the big estate house had just moved out. Dick had already told her about our family and that we had 15 horses. Hearing that, she said we could move in immediately and that we could also bring our horses.

When I asked what the rent was for the barn and pasture, she replied, "Would $500 a month for the house and $250 for the barn and pasture be okay?" The going rate for boarding one horse in the area was $300 a month. I was in shock and replied that her offer would be fine.

CHAPTER 3

Ride our horses for miles

I COULDN'T WAIT TO CALL Margie with the news.

The estate home, which resembled something out of the movie "Money Pit," was overgrown with ivy so thick that to enter by the front door I needed to duck down.

The electrical wiring was also messed up. Eventually, she had the ivy cut down, and the house repainted and the electrical repaired.

In walking the property, it was evident this had at one time been a very impressive estate. There were horse trails connecting the estates throughout the area and we could ride our horses for miles.

We made multiple trips from Tulsa to Boston. On our first trip to Boston, we took our tractor, and some equipment so I could start putting up fencing and fix up the barn. We made five or six trips, taking two horses at a time, from Tulsa to Boston.

Thankfully, the school moved most of our personal items.

One fall day, Margie, Allison, Jeff and I took a ride on the trails through fall colors so vivid they almost took your breath away. As we rode on this crisp fall day, a flock of white geese, contrasted against a bright blue sky, were honking loudly in a "V" formation as they migrated south.

Everything was in perfect harmony, and I thought, *Lord, this is a glimpse of heaven; may I never forget this moment*, and I never have.

The house was like a museum with a large attic containing numerous antiques and a two-story library the size of a basketball half-court containing many first edition volumes from as early as the 1700s.

Later, Mrs. Phillips donated all those books, with an estimated value of over a million dollars, to Gordon College. Topsfield's first horse-drawn fire engine was in the library with a number of other intriguing items. The house also had a three-bedroom, one bathroom maid's quarters where Jeff Reinke lived.

The Boston area is where our country was founded. The New England area is filled with history and we made a point of visiting as many sites as we could.

For example, we visited the Plymouth Plantation on Cape Cod where actors reenact the lives of the people who arrived on the Mayflower. The actors lived on the site and played the characters that originally lived there. We went into the home of William Bradford, the leader of the colony.

The actress playing Bradford's wife was cooking when Margie asked her, "Does your husband help with the dishes?" The woman looked at her in shocked disbelief and said, "Are you crazy? He's out hunting and providing for the family."

One memorable event was seeing the movie *Ben-Hur* at the Wang Theater in downtown Boston on a 70-foot screen. It was hosted by the movie's lead, Charlton Heston. On the way there, Allison and Jeff complained about having to go to an "old" movie.

Afterward, we all agreed it was the best movie experience we'd ever had. In 1959 *Ben-Hur* won a record 11 Academy awards and Charlton Heston won Best Actor.

It remains our family's favorite movie.

CHAPTER 4

A mound of snow

THE HOUSE WAS HEATED by a large boiler connected to three 300-gallon oil-filled tanks. Located in the basement, the boiler was huge, nearly as big as the basement itself.

By November, it started getting really cold so we did what we normally did and turned up the thermostat.

The house was filled with steam radiators that worked pretty well in heating the entire house. Our heating-oil supplier knew we were from the West and thought they should check on the oil consumption after the cold spell. The tanks were nearly empty. We had used 900 gallons in one month.

At a buck a gallon, our bill for one month was $900.

Whoa. We've got to make some changes.

We bought a big wood stove that we placed in the big fireplace in the living room. I cut down a huge dead white oak tree, and split enough wood for the entire year using a motorized log splitter. We covered all the windows with plastic wrap and closed off most of the house.

It was a breezy, cold house, so we bought electric space heaters for our bedrooms.

Now we understood why the previous family was called the "Parka" family. We ended up wearing our parkas in the house as well.

During the winters, we had to trudge through two or three feet of snow just to get to the barn and feed the horses. The water buckets would be frozen, and we had to knock the ice out of them, morning and night, until we got some heaters for the water.

Of course, we brought our two dogs with us.

Joe Buck was a yellow lab and Jedi was a 130-pound Kuvasz, a Hungarian breed that was bred to protect cavalry horses. The estate was heaven for the dogs. Joe Buck was an outdoor dog, but when it was cold, he stayed inside.

On the other hand, Jedi had a thick coat and loved the cold.

One night, it was well below zero, so we put him in an area off our kitchen. The next morning when we woke up and came to the kitchen, it was freezing and Jedi was missing. He had jumped up, broken the window of the door, and climbed outside.

When we found him, he was laying contentedly on a mound of snow.

There was one road and two entrances to the estate. One entrance wound through a grove of trees near a good-sized pond that had been used for making blocks of ice and ice-skating. The other entrance was through a very large pasture.

Big as it was, the house could not be seen from either entrance.

CHAPTER 5

Turning it around

GORDON COLLEGE IS A CHRISTIAN INSTITUTION with very high academic standards. The campus sits on about 40 of the 300 acres that are owned by the college, including a large pond surrounded by trees, near the campus.

Witches' covens continue to exist in the area, and many times, they found evidence of animal sacrifices on campus property. At that time, Gordon had the largest percentage of students contemplating suicide of any Christian campus in the country.

I was about to experience first-hand what Jeff Reinke had mentioned, that there was a lot of spiritual warfare occurring in the area.

When I heard that the basketball program had suffered 17 straight years of losing records, I knew that turning it around would be a huge challenge. The soccer program had a good coach and was successful, but the other sports needed a great deal of help.

Plus, the sports facilities were sub-standard, way behind the school's high academics.

Gordon's president, Dick Gross, was a former basketball player at Wheaton College. He was an extremely good administrator and became a very good friend. He belonged to the exclusive Miopia Golf and Polo Club that had fewer than 100 members, and we played lots of golf there over the years.

I'll never forget one round we had with one of his sons. I was approaching the tee to hit my drive, and Dick had his arm around his son and said, "It doesn't get any better than this."

I'll never forget that moment of his joy of playing with his son. That inspired me to do the same with my children.

———— ∞∞∞ ————

I had hired Dolph Carroll, who had been fired by Ted Owens at ORU around the same time I was fired, to be my assistant coach. Dolph and his new bride lived with us until they found another place to rent.

Before Dolph came to Gordon, I got a call from him saying that Osaro Onaiwu, who was playing for ORU, was desperate. He had been transferred from ORU to a junior college in the Oklahoma panhandle, and said he was being held against his will, unable to leave his dorm.

After Dolph asked me what we could do, I told him to get Osaro out of his dorm and that I'd see if we could get him into Gordon College.

After Dolph arrived, Osaro climbed out his dorm window and Dolph drove him back to Tulsa. I did manage to get him accepted to Gordon, and a few days later he moved into one of the dorms.

Just after his arrival at Gordon, our family took Osaro to a Fourth of July concert on a huge park that borders the Charles River. The concert was performed with fireworks by the Boston Pops. It was quite an experience for our family, and especially for Osaro.

After a year at Gordon, Dolph got the assistant coaching job at Northern Arizona University, a D-1 school, and took Osaro with him. While I would miss them both, I was glad for them.

Over the next three years, Gordon agreed to increase the athletic department's budget in any way I believed would be beneficial to the program. I wanted to invest the money in good quality people I could trust and work well with.

After a year, the president gave me his own administrative secretary to be my athletic secretary. She understood quickly who I was, what my abilities were, and what I wanted to accomplish.

I would tell her what I needed, and she got it done. It got to the point where she knew what I needed before I even asked.

She was a tremendous gift, and I was grateful to Dick for her.

The women's volleyball team had never had a winning season, and their last season they were 9–18. Jeff Reinke found he had some good, dedicated athletes, even though they lacked fundamentals.

Jeff recruited a 6-1 center from the basketball team who had never played volleyball to be a middle blocker on the volleyball team. That season, she became the team's most valuable player.

As a coach, Jeff spent an inordinate amount of time teaching fundamentals. He taught what I had always emphasized, that the foundation of all sports is balance and footwork, plus the volleyball basics of passing, serving and hitting the ball accurately.

He put in a simple, basic system of defense and offense, and emphasized the importance of making fewer mistakes than your opponent.

I had only been a head coach for three years, and an assistant for two, and Jeff had never been a head coach. So, we were basically learning as we went along. He did an unbelievable job, and the team was 34–1, and made the NAIA playoffs for their first time ever.

Incredible.

The situation at Gordon was very similar to what I had experienced at UCSD. We were both members of the NAIA that offered athletic scholarships. However, Gordon and UCSD were non-scholarship schools, so we were at a tremendous disadvantage.

Once again, we were "the win" on another team's schedule, AKA a cupcake.

Scholastically, Gordon was considered a Christian equivalent of Harvard. Student/athletes had to be good academically, as well as good players, and have faith in God. Not having athletic scholarships made things even more difficult.

As I had done at UCSD, I got the administration to apply for membership in the NCAA D-3, since there were many D-3 schools within a two-hour driving radius of Boston.

After our admission to the NCAA, I started a conversation with other athletic directors and basketball coaches to form a new league. After a few months, the Commonwealth Coast Conference came into existence.

CHAPTER 6

Struggling mightily

THAT FIRST BASKETBALL SEASON was less than stellar. We played a schedule set up by the previous athletic director, and we were consistently overmatched.

As I had during my first season at UCSD, I wanted to find out who the toughest competitors were on our team. As a result, we ended up with only eight players on the team, after starting with 15.

This would become the norm with the schools I coached. I wanted to build a culture of hard, intense, focused play that was done in every practice. We went 9–17 that year.

The following year we recruited well and brought in some tough-minded kids. Before the school year began, I got a call from a mother who told me that her son Mike played basketball with Eastern Nazarene College until he was asked to leave. She had heard of me and thought I would be a good coach for him.

I said I'd be happy to meet with her and discuss his situation. He happened to be one of the four sons of Rico Petrocelli, the legendary third baseman for the Boston Red Sox.

Mike came to play for me, but he was struggling mightily. He was a gifted 6-7 athlete, but he'd get so angry at himself that at times he couldn't perform to his capabilities.

One day he came to my office and said, "I was sitting with this girl and suddenly I began going into a depression that led to thoughts of suicide. I don't know what to do."

I told him that I believed it was demonic.

I said, "Mike, when you start feeling yourself going down, excuse yourself, go back to your room, open your Bible and start reading it out loud." He said, "Okay."

Demons cannot read your mind. They only know what you might be thinking through your words and actions. That is why I wanted Mike to read his Bible and pray out loud.

He told me later, "I was sitting with this girl again when I started going into depression and the idea of suicide came on me again. I got up and excused myself, went to my room and started reading my Bible aloud. I kind of went to sleep and had a dream."

He had a vision of two girls on their knees praying for him. He had no idea how long he was asleep when he heard a hard knock on the door. It was the two girls in his dream, and they said, "We've been praying for you. What's going on with you?"

He told them and they all prayed together.

He was learning that through the Word of God that he could control his responses to his thoughts. He still wasn't playing well because of his anger with himself when he made mistakes.

One day he was in my office, and I asked him, "Mike, tell me what's going on."

I had learned through being a coach that most, maybe all, of the emotional problems males and females have stem primarily with their relationship with their dads. I asked him, "Mike, what's your relationship with your dad?" He said it wasn't good.

I said, "Mike, do you want to get rid of all this anger?"

"I'll do anything," he replied.

"Here's what you do," I told him. "Get on that phone right now and call your dad and say, 'I'm coming home. I want to meet with you.' Ask for his forgiveness for having anger toward him. You need to confess it to the Lord and to him."

Mike met with his father and his family the next night. After the meeting, his mother called me and said, "Thank you for what you did for Mike. It's changed him and our whole family. All the kids were able to express their thoughts about their dad and we're now reconciled."

Mike became a new man, changed virtually right on the spot. He rarely expressed anger any longer and played two more years as an outstanding, tough-minded player.

I believe that evil exists in our world, but in church and youth group, we don't emphasize enough that we're engaged in spiritual warfare. We've become soft. It's all about how we feel.

In my view, we not only have to feel, we must *know*. We must know what the Word of God has to say and live it out.

It's warfare.

The demonic world doesn't want us to know that the devil is at war with God. In the Bible, Jesus addresses this precept and he himself casts out demons. Just because some people don't believe in spiritual warfare doesn't mean the demons don't exist.

CHAPTER 7

A great deal of demonic activity

In the summer of 1990, our family was on vacation in California, where I got in contact with my friend, Mike Dodd. He and his wife, who was also a top volleyball player, lived in Manhattan Beach.

I asked him if he could coach Allison and set her up to play in Manhattan Beach, a beach volleyball hotbed. He agreed and invited us to stay in his home for a while.

Allison discovered that there was a volleyball camp at UC Santa Barbara led by their coach Kathy Gregory, a former the No. 1-ranked beach volleyball player and All-America basketball player.

Allison wanted to go to the camp, but it was scheduled after her 16th birthday, and I needed to be back at Gordon by then. Allison asked me if she could stay in Manhattan Beach and live at her cousin's apartment to continue playing beach volleyball and attend the camp.

I was in agreement, but Margie didn't like the idea at all. We would miss our daughter's 16th birthday and leave her for about two weeks. I told Margie I believed that we could trust our daughter and I would prepare her for this experience. She would live with her cousin Carolyn in Manhattan Beach.

Having lived and played a lot of volleyball in that area myself, I knew the culture well.

Allison was a good-looking, athletic young woman. I told her specifically how the young men were going to look at her, what they would be thinking, and how they would be talking to her.

I took her to the airport and walked her through the whole process of flying from checking in to getting to the gates. I showed her how to take a bus back and forth to Santa Barbara before returning to LAX to fly back home.

The only condition was that Allison had to call us every night, which she did.

Not long after she returned home, she got a call from a young man whom she had met playing volleyball. He was very interested in her, and since he was driving his sister to college on the East Coast, he wanted to come up and see her.

When she told me, I sat with her and expressed the different possibilities of his motivation. I told her to watch how he responded to first meeting me and to listen carefully to his words and how he treated her.

He took her to dinner and when she returned, she said she told him there was no reason for him to stick around.

As I mentioned earlier, Gordon had the most students contemplating suicide of any Christian College in the nation. It got so bad they had to hire extra counselors. I experienced a great deal of demonic activity myself while at Gordon, including the following two events.

After practice one evening, I came home and entered the kitchen where Margie was fixing dinner. I sat down at the table. Life was good, but completely out of the blue, the thought crossed my mind: *Life is not worth living. I should just kill myself.*

Nothing like this had ever entered my mind, before or since. I left the kitchen immediately, went upstairs to our bedroom and laid down without saying a word to Margie. This was so uncharacteristic of me that she came up right away and asked if everything was okay.

I said no, it wasn't, and asked her to pray for me. When she prayed, those thoughts immediately left, never to return.

Another time was at an away game at Anna Maria College, in Worcester, Massachusetts. The gym was packed, the crowd was boisterous, and when the game started it was like sleeping dust had fallen on my team. We just couldn't get it going, meaning we were playing awful.

I used to wear a coat and tie on the sidelines. I was so angry that at one point in the game I ripped off my coat splitting the back seam, and threw it on the floor. A little later I ripped off my tie, tearing the buttons off my shirt. That was the most out of control I have ever been in my life.

We were a much better team, but we lost by a couple of points. In the locker room after the game, I said to my team, "All I need is some ash, for that was an abomination."

Since I had already torn my clothes, as Biblical Jews did, that was my very weak attempt at humor, which the players didn't get anyway.

CHAPTER 8

Tormented anguish

WE WERE ON THE NEW JERSEY TURNPIKE, just starting a two-hour drive back to Gordon in a school van and my own Suburban. I was still seething inside when I turned in my seat and yelled at my players that they were not to listen to their Walkmans in my presence ever again.

I went to the van behind us and said the same thing. I was still angry, but no longer crazy. Whenever I walked on campus and saw one of them listening to a Walkman, they immediately removed their headphones.

I told them later that when they were on campus with their headphones on, it was perceived that they didn't want to be bothered.

When I got home from dropping the players off, it was around 1:30 in the morning. I immediately got undressed and got in bed. Margie was awake and asked how things went. I said, "Okay," and tried to go to sleep.

I was so tormented in my spirit that I jumped out of bed and went into the shower to calm myself down. When I was in the shower, I screamed in tormented anguish. Margie came in and asked what was going on.

I simply replied, "Pray for me."

She returned to bed and began praying for me. Immediately, the torment left, and I physically sighed with relief and relaxed. I had just learned a monumental life lesson. I had lost control of my mind and opened myself up to the influence of demons.

One afternoon, while I was in my office, my son Jeff and Jeff Reinke were in the gym when I heard a huge crash. I already knew a worker and one of my players were cleaning a furnace in the gym, 30 feet above the floor.

I ran to the gym to see what had happened. The scaffolding they had been standing on had fallen over.

The worker was unconscious, in a heap on the floor. My player was hanging by his fingers, 30 feet in the air, screaming for help. I was filled with adrenaline and almost supernatural strength. I immediately went to the scaffolding and started lifting it upright, by myself, screaming for others to help me.

Jeff Reinke and some others ran over to help me finish standing the scaffolding up. We then walked it over to the player who was able to climb back onto it. The worker on the floor was seriously injured with numerous broken bones and a brain injury.

He never fully recovered.

CHAPTER 9

Everything was black

GORDON COLLEGE FREQUENTLY HOSTED concerts in the gym, including one I attended with my family that featured a very impressive Christian rock group from Russia known as RUSCHA.

They sang a memorable song with lyrics taken from Isaiah 40:8: "The grass withers, the flower fades, but the word of the Lord stands forever."

One morning around 6, I got a call from the fire chief from Wenham telling me to get down to the gym immediately. There had been a fire in my office. While walking carefully to the gym over snow and ice, I was met by the fire chief, who was a Gordon graduate and played noon basketball with us.

He told me that the janitor came in that morning to clean the gym and saw smoke coming from my office door. He called security, and as the guard arrived, the janitor was opening the door. The security guard immediately pulled him away, which may have saved the janitor's life.

As the door opened, the entire office exploded in fire. A faulty space heater I had accidentally left on had ignited the carpet.

As we were walking in the gym toward my office, the fire chief said, "You're not going to believe what you're about to see."

I had a large office with a metal desk with files and various papers, and a metal credenza with my Mac computer on it. I had a bookcase filled with books and on the wall was my basketball personal memorabilia, including my NBA All-Star plaque and photos.

When I entered the office, everything was black. There was no couch or chairs, no carpet, and everything that had been on the wall was now ash on the floor. My desk was covered in ash, and my computer on the credenza was melted.

Next to my computer was my NIV Study Bible, still sitting there, untouched by the fire. That and my pocket Bible were the only items to survive the fire. It was not lost on me that my "wall of pride" was totally destroyed, but the Word of God was not.

When I got home later and told my family what had happened, my kids in unison said, "The grass withers, the flower fades, but the word of the Lord will stand forever."

Harold L. Busséll was Gordon's school chaplain and had been among the top organists in the country. He never played in public or in church because he didn't want the church organist to compare her talent with his.

Sometime later, I was invited to his home to hear him, and his playing was majestic. He had graduated from Bethany College, a small Christian school just outside Santa Cruz, California.

Harold had never concentrated on athletics, but he wanted to connect with athletes. He was small in stature and began going to the gym, lifting weights. Though he wasn't very athletic, he soon became so dedicated that he turned into a body-builder.

Our family attended the Congregational Church where he was pastor. On one hot, humid day, the church was steaming. When Harold got up to preach with his black robe on, he was dripping with sweat. He apologized to the congregation and said he needed to remove his robe.

When he did, the entire congregation gasped when they saw their surprisingly muscle-bound pastor in his tight white shirt.

PART 19

Travels to Spain

CHAPTER 1

Step out of your comfort zone

As Gordon College's athletic director, I was considered a faculty member and so was invited to participate in a small faculty group Bible study.

We were studying the Sermon on the Mount in Matthew, and each week a different member taught on different verses. There was a lot of frustration among the members in trying to figure out what the beatitudes meant and how to live up to that standard.

The section I was to teach came from the passage where Jesus said we are salt and light, and I read several commentaries to prepare for my presentation.

I'd been praying a lot and found the beatitudes revealed the character of God. I would study them and the rest of that sermon extensively for the rest of my life. If believers in Jesus want to grasp the foundation of their faith, it can be found in the Sermon on the Mount.

In the midst of my teaching, God spoke to my spirit saying, "Do you really want my character?" I answered "yes" while I was still speaking to the group. He said, "Then step out of your comfort zone and rely on me."

I stopped and told the professors what God was telling me. There was no response.

After the study, I hurriedly walked down to my office and called my friend, Eddie Waxer. A Jew who had come to know the Lord Jesus, Eddie had been given the vision of an international sports ministry. I had met him years earlier at a tennis camp at Oakbridge through Stan Smith.

I told Eddie what had happened at the Bible study and that God had told me to get out of my comfort zone. I asked him, "Where's the toughest place in the world to share Jesus? I want to go there." He said, "I think that's pretty easy — Spain."

That surprised me, and I said, "Okay, Eddie, I want to take a team there. Let's set it up."

That was in the spring of 1988. My next call was to Al Nordquist, asking him if he was willing to travel to Spain with me. We only had a few months to put together the whole trip.

The logistics of finding players, booking travel, finding uniforms, and raising money was daunting.

Eddie set the trip up, and by the summer of 1988, Al and I took a team to Spain. At 44, I was one of the eight players on the team. Al, who coached the team, took a player from Moorpark College and one of his former players, a tremendous guard, Steve Abraham, who is now a pastor of a large church in Oxnard, California.

I took two players from Gordon, Mike Petrocelli and Doug Rotondi.

Amazingly, we were able to raise the money to go to Spain in a very short time. Al got some old Moorpark College Raiders uniforms for the team, and in Spain we became known as "Los Raiders."

We were hosted by Antonio Pardo, whom Eddie said was highly regarded as the Billy Graham of Spain. Antonio had been a professional soccer player and now led a national ministry. He set us up to travel throughout the small towns in Southern Spain, where we would play against various town teams.

We flew into Málaga and drove to Rincón de La Victoria, where Antonio's home and ministry were located.

We played our first game on an undersized outdoor court overlooking the ocean, with very few stands and about 40 or 50 people in attendance. Our opponent was from an 18-year-and-under club team named the Maristas.

They were good and they narrowly beat us for our only loss in our three trips to Spain.

We had given our testimonies of our faith in Jesus at halftime, and after the game a lady approached me to say she wanted to help in some way. She thought it was a shame that such a good game was played on this little court.

Then she pointed to a hill and said she owned some property there. She asked me what I thought she could do with it. I told her that maybe a church could be built and used as a town community center, where basketball could be played.

I wondered whether her dream would ever come true.

CHAPTER 2

Jacked up on adrenaline

WE VISITED SIX OR SEVEN TOWNS in the coal-mining and wine country regions in Southern Spain.

All of them had populations of fewer than 30,000 and had basketball programs, as well as a missionary evangelist. But there were many who had not seen anyone come to Christ in many years.

Still, they remained faithful to the call from God that had brought them there. As we traveled from town to town, I began seeing that these missionaries were categorized as evangelicals by the traditional religious leaders. They had been marginalized because of their theology.

I was starting to see what Eddie Waxer meant when he said that Spain was the most difficult place in the world to share the gospel.

In contrast to our first game, the crowds were huge, and we were enthusiastically received. We did clinics and played games on outdoor and indoor courts. The crowds enthusiastically cheered every point by both teams. I told my team that the excitement was a glimpse into what it was like for me in the NBA.

At halftime, a few of the players and I shared our testimonies.

One game, I took my Bible that had been miraculously preserved in the office fire. I told the story to the crowd, and afterward I was surrounded by those who wanted to touch my Bible.

Our three weeks in Spain was amazing because God opened many doors.

In Puente Genil, the town was really excited about us being there. The Los Raiders were coming to town! We met the mayor and were interviewed on the local radio station.

Antonio had these pamphlets printed that on the cover read in Spanish, "The Best Have Also Fallen." The pamphlet contained my testimony, along with that of Al Nordquist and some of our players.

Within the pamphlet was a booklet that contained the Gospel of John. Antonio had printed 1,000 copies, but we ran out of them so quickly that he had to print several thousand more. We were rushed by crowds asking us to autograph them.

Our games were always played later in the evening, around 10. Then we'd have dinner with the mayors and other officials, but not until midnight or later, which is common in Spain.

We soon realized that we were in Spain to help Antonio present the gospel, set a good standard of basketball, and help empower the missionaries in these communities. In one town, the missionary had not seen one person come to faith in Jesus Christ in eight years.

We helped connect him to his community by having him translate wherever we went, at all of the basketball clinics, and for our halftime testimonies.

At the dinner afterward with the mayor and other community leaders, I had the missionary sit next to me to translate. I encouraged them to get to know this missionary and encouraged the missionary to invest his time meeting with the leaders.

I also suggested he get to know the parish priest, study the Bible, and pray with him.

The food in Spain was outstanding, especially the *paella,* and the ice cream was the best I've ever enjoyed. It was so good that I gained almost 20 pounds on that trip.

CHAPTER 3

'Put me in, coach'

TWO YEARS LATER, JUST BEFORE our second trip to Spain in 1990, Margie challenged me to see if I was disciplined enough to go the entire trip without having one bite of ice cream.

I must admit that I'd gained a lot of weight.

I said yes, and then told Al Nordquist what Margie had said and that he would be my witness. Early on, it was a struggle, but I soon fell into a good rhythm of saying no.

When we got to Spain, our team had the NAIA scoring champion, and the NCAA Western Regional MVP, who played center for Arizona. We had a very good team, and the competition improved as we played in bigger towns.

As before, we started in Rincón de La Victoria. I asked Antonio how the property was coming along, and he said the lady with whom I had spoken on our previous trip had donated the property. Plans had been drawn up with a design for the church to also be used as a community center with a basketball court.

Everything was ready to go, but the church and Antonio were having problems getting approval by the town.

I told Antonio to set up a meeting with the mayor, so Antonio, Al, and I met with the mayor and his staff. I cast the vision to the mayor that the church and the town become partners in building both a church and a community center.

"Okay, we'll get it done," he said, and the plans were later approved.

One of our games really stands out, when we played a team in Coín toward the end of our trip in a good-sized arena. Los Raiders had been so successful that the Coín team had added two pro Spanish players, a center and a guard.

When the game started, it was evident this was going to be a battle. Our center from Arizona was not able to handle their big center, so I told Al, "Put me in, Coach. I'm gonna shut this kid down."

I was 46 years old, and I did shut the kid down. I schooled him on offense with moves and fakes he had probably never seen before. I got him to foul me, so I shot a lot of free throws.

I was so jacked up on adrenaline that I even tried to dunk on him, and he fouled me. We shocked the other team by winning, and the crowd loved it.

After the game, two men in suits asked me to meet with them in the morning. At the meeting, they told me they owned the professional team in Coín. They offered me a large contract to play for them, but only in home games.

That really surprised me, and I was honored, but I told them I was an athletic director and basketball coach of a college in the States. Besides, I had a family, so there was no way I could accept their offer.

CHAPTER 4

Now a flourishing reality

WHEN WE RETURNED TO SPAIN for the third time, in 1992, I was coaching at Bethany College.

I took along some players from Bethany, along with my daughter Allison and two young women students from the college. Steve Abraham went with us again, after missing the second trip.

Of the trip's many highlights, one was attending the World's Fair in Seville. Allison and I went to the Canadian pavilion, where there was a 360-degree movie screen featuring video highlights of Canada.

One segment featured a flyover video of the Malibu Young Life Camp, where I had run basketball camps two years in a row with my friends Jim Barnett, along with Paul and Bill Westphal. It was a real joy to have Allison get an up-close view of the camp.

The other highlight was seeing the first phase of the Parque Victoria church on the property that had been donated. The vision was in the process of being fulfilled, and continues to this day. Al, Steve, Antonio and I were part of that first trip and the church's genesis, and we were rejoicing with Antonio and that first congregation.

Thirty years after our first trip, in 2018, people in the towns we had visited in Southern Spain were asking, to my surprise, about John Block. Some of those whom we had influenced on our three trips had become pastors and missionaries.

Through them and Ruben Fernandez, who had traveled with us on our first trip, we were invited to do a reunion tour of some of those towns.

Without hesitation and with tremendous excitement, Steve, Al and I said yes. What excited me the most was that Margie was coming with me and would see the fruits of our labors in Spain.

We were told that we were one of the reasons that basketball now flourished in Southern Spain. Now, there are professional leagues throughout the region, which has become a major influence in the growth of Spanish basketball.

We laid the groundwork, and God was the architect.

We again met with town mayors, missionaries, and pastors. Steve encouraged them and shared the Gospel. By the grace of God, despite my physical limitations, I did 19 hours of clinics in four days with a lot of energy.

Toward the end of the trip, Steve, Margie and I returned to Rincón de La Victoria. What began in 1988 as a vision is now a flourishing reality. One of the largest evangelical churches in Southern Spain, Parque Victoria church has also become a community center.

At a Sunday service, I was able to share the origin of their church with the congregation, and Steve preached a powerful sermon.

This trip began a celebration of 50 years of our marriage. We continued the celebration with a flight from Málaga to Rome for a two-week cruise through the Mediterranean, including visiting Israel.

We traveled with Dick and Sharon Whipple and Bob and Barbara Diller, the parents of my daughter's husband. We had all traveled together before, and really enjoyed each other's company.

Dick said one of the conditions for them going on the trip was that I would baptize him in the Jordan River. I agreed, but only if he baptized me. That baptism was one of my life's most unforgettable moments.

PART 20

Back to Gordon

CHAPTER 1

A trip they would never forget

WHEN I WAS IN HARLEM, the head of Young Life on the Lower East Side of New York was an African-American named Bo Nixon. He wanted to bring two African-American high school students who were basketball players to Gordon to visit the campus and spend some time with me.

The four of us met in my office and in the course of our conversation I said we were sitting on holy ground because the Lord was in my office. Our conversation centered more on what God's role was in our lives than on our basketball and college experiences.

Through that conversation an idea emerged to put together a Young Life inner-city basketball tournament, bringing in teams from different areas. The first tournament was held at Gordon and was like a mini-Young Life camp.

During spring break, we hosted six teams from New York, Massachusetts, New Jersey, and Rhode Island. We were bringing in 40 to 50 inner-city kids to live in student dorms. Understandably, there was some concern, but not from President Gross. He loved it.

The tournament went extremely well and there were no incidents at all. The Young Life leaders did a great job in preparing these kids for these camps.

It went so well that the next year we expanded the program and went to the larger Young Life camp, held in Lake Champion in New York.

Young Life has a highly successful way of putting a camp together and sharing the Gospel of Jesus Christ. Many kids who go through those camps will say that it is one of the best weeks of their lives. It's something to see and always very special.

I wanted all my teams to have a trip they would never forget, so prior to our 1987–'88 season, I scheduled several games in Orlando, Florida.

While our team members and my son Jeff were at Disney World, I called Margie on a payphone. I was shocked to hear that my former teammate and friend, the legendary "Pistol" Pete Maravich, had died.

He was scheduled to be a guest on a Focus on the Family broadcast, hosted by James Dobson. The day before, at the old Pasadena Nazarene Church gym, Dobson, Gary Lydic and others including UCLA's Ralph Drollinger, had played some pickup games.

After one of the games as they were walking to get a drink of water, Gary said, "Pete, you can still really play!" Pete responded, "Yeah, I feel great!" He immediately collapsed and everyone there thought he was joking. Before he hit the ground, he was dead at age 40.

Pete was still young and just getting started in the ministry God had called him to. The autopsy revealed he had a heart defect that few people live with beyond the age of 22.

CHAPTER 2

Like an Angel was Playing

I DON'T RECALL HOW I FIRST CONNECTED with Brian Walker, but as a coach I was known for giving players second, and even third, chances.

I believe Brian had been to another college but hadn't played basketball for a while. He contacted me and after we had a good conversation, he came to play at Gordon as a junior. He was a really good learner, and a strong 6-6 player.

His father was black and a good athlete and he was living with his mother who was white.

One day Brian invited our family to his church where he and his mom, Gail, were very involved. The first Sunday that Margie and I went there, Gail had us sit in the front row with her.

Paul and Mona Johnian were the pastors, and after the service Paul approached me and asked if I would give my testimony at their Monday night service. I found this unusual since we had just met. Our family started attending the church, and our lives would never be the same.

We had been to all-white churches and all-black churches, but this was strikingly different.

The church was racially diverse with people attending from all socio-economic backgrounds. The church met in Woburn, Massachusetts, was about an hour's drive for us. It was well worth the drive.

Paul and Mona are a unique couple. Paul was raised in the Boston area, and Mona was raised in the hills of Tennessee. Paul had studied violin under the famous Spanish violin teacher, Andrés Segovia, in Puerto Rico. As I understand it, Paul was first violin of the World Symphony.

Paul and Mona met in Puerto Rico, got married and were led to start a church in the Boston area. His gifts are preaching and evangelism, and her gifts are teaching the Bible and prophecy.

Their daughter, who had never really sung before, was being led by the Holy Spirit to lead worship and was given the gift of a beautiful voice.

Occasionally, Paul would accompany the worship team with his violin. When he did, it was like an angel was playing. Or maybe like King David. They had a Monday evening service, so that those who went to a different church on Sunday could attend.

One Monday evening service is etched into our memories. After the preaching, Mona got up and started walking around the room prophesying over certain people, and encouraging them.

When it looked like she was finishing, Paul got out his violin, walked across the room and knelt beside a woman in an aisle seat. There, he began playing different renditions of "Jesus loves me, this I know, for the Bible tells me so..."

He got up and simply said, "Jesus loves you." He put his violin in his case and sat down. Every person in the building had tears in their eyes.

CHAPTER 3

The cheerleaders were in tears

As I mentioned previously, I believe that sports is basically entertainment, and that it's supposed to be enjoyable for participants and fans.

That thought in mind, I put together a Gordon College cheerleading squad. I encouraged them to come up with various cultural and historical themes, with Western and the Roaring '20s among them.

When hard playing is combined with a winning team and an entertaining half-time experience, fans love it. That's exactly what happened. Eventually we would pack the Gordon College gym every night. We put together a group of young women who were dedicated and excited to do something original and creative.

Wearing costumes, they choreographed routines that they asked me to critique in advance.

We had a big game and the stands were packed. Paul and Mona Johnian, Brian Walker's mother, Gail, and some members of their congregation were in attendance. After winning the game, I came out of the locker room and back into the gym. There, I saw Gail talking to the cheerleaders.

The following day, with tears in their eyes they explained to me what Gail had said. She had told them they were too risqué and not honoring God. They were devastated, and I was pretty bummed. That soured my relationship with her for a short time.

I had a long talk with the cheerleaders who said they didn't want to offend anyone. I had videotaped the halftime routine in question, and we decided to dial the movements back a bit. They put together another routine to be performed at the next home game and had me critique it. I told them that it looked good.

During the next home game, we played an easy team. Instead of talking to my team at halftime, I stayed out to watch the cheerleaders. It was a packed crowd when the head cheerleader went on the microphone and apologized to the fans for any offense that might have been taken from their previous routines.

After the game, Gail ripped the cheerleaders again, saying it still wasn't good enough.

Gail and I were not talking, even at church. I was praying about this very difficult situation when the Lord gave me a scripture, Romans: 14:1, *"Accept the one who is weak, without quarrelling over disputable matters."*

That changed my thinking toward her.

Before the next home game, I called Gail aside and said, "We need to talk." First of all, I told her that I was very disappointed with what she did and said to the girls. I told her that they were responsible to me, that I had been overseeing them. If she had a beef with them, she needed to come to me.

I let her know the cheerleaders were in tears because they didn't measure up to her standard. I told her what the Lord had revealed to me through Romans 14:1 and that she was causing these women to stumble.

It was a marvelous time because she received what I said and apologized. We were both humbled and got back on track. The situation was never discussed again and our relationship was restored. It was quite a lesson for me.

I had prayed and received God's thoughts and wisdom through scripture.

CHAPTER 4

Risky for all of us

IN THE BEGINNING OF MY FIFTH YEAR at Gordon, I decided to get a master's degree in Organization and Management at Antioch University. It was a cohort program, meaning it was a small group of students, designed for people who worked full-time.

It was a two-year program that I wanted to do in one year. They offered classes two nights a week in a classroom in Portsmouth, New Hampshire, which was a 30-minute drive. There were also various weekend classes to fulfill the required units.

My cohort consisted of six women and me. They were all professionals and one of them was the head of the National Education Association (NEA) in the area.

The classes were taught by two Antioch professors, a man and a woman, who told me their class might pose a difficult challenge for me.

It seems they thought my Biblical worldview was quite different from that of my cohorts.

After we had been together for a while, I got a call one night from the professors saying we would be doing a classic Values Clarification exercise called "Lifeboat." They said it could be challenging and very risky for all of us.

The next evening at class they explained the Lifeboat exercise. They had set up a room with masking tape on the floor in the shape of a boat. We were to get into the boat that was about to sink in 30 minutes into shark-infested waters unless one person went overboard.

I sat in the "boat" with my classmates, discussing who would go overboard, with very little input from me. There were only two minutes before the boat sank and we weren't close to making a decision. The professors were counting down the time and just before the boat was to sink, I left the boat.

Everyone was so shocked that the professors ended the class. I got a call from the professors the night before the next class. They said that my classmates were very upset with me and that I should be prepared for a heated discussion.

No problem, but I prayed a lot.

At our next class, the professors warned me that the students were upset at not having a say in my decision. They asked me to come up front and tell the six women what was behind my decision.

Safely behind a podium, I explained that after all our discussion and deliberation, time was running out. We were all going to die if someone didn't leave the boat. I said that I was a believer in God, and that Jesus taught that greater love has no man than to lay down his life for his friends.

Everyone was speechless.

From then on, we became trusted friends instead of merely classmates.

For the last class of the year, the professors asked us to bring a prop to express our class experience. I took the train to Boston to a store known for its collection of posters. When it was my turn to speak, I unrolled the poster of King Kong holding Fay Raye atop the Empire State Building.

Everyone burst into laughter.

We had come a long way from that first day in class.

From that experience I continued learning how valuable it is to pray about everything and let the Lord direct. I was learning to listen patiently and respond thoughtfully, expressing in some measure the fruit of the Holy Spirit.

Boy, do I need to be reminded of that.

That was an exhilarating, but challenging time for me. I had my family and our horses, and I was athletic director, basketball coach and a full-time student — all at the same time.

At times, I was so focused that it was ridiculous. I would have my books on my car seat so that if I stopped at a stoplight, I could get in one or two minutes of reading.

I came within two classes of getting my master's, but God had another direction for me.

CHAPTER 5

Praying for a clear message

ONE OF PETE MARAVICH'S PASSIONS was helping single moms with their kids. Focus on the Family started a single-mom kids weekend basketball camp in Pete's honor.

My friend, Gary Lydic, got in touch with me about having a Pete Maravich camp at Gordon College, and I readily agreed. I had traveled with Pete after he got to know the Lord, and we held that camp during my last year at Gordon.

His best friend was John Lotz, whom I got to know through Pete. John was an associate athletic director at the University of North Carolina (UNC), a former assistant coach with the legendary Dean Smith, and a very successful head coach at the University of Florida.

He also was the brother-in-law of Anne Graham Lotz, Billy Graham's daughter, and was a deeply committed follower of Jesus.

John was one of the coaches at the Maravich camp, along with Phil Oates, the coach and athletic director from Bethany College in Northern California, just outside Santa Cruz. Little did I know those two relationships would soon take me across the country, back to the West Coast.

In my discussions with John at the camp, I told him that my daughter Allison was being recruited to East Coast colleges for her volleyball talent. But she wanted to go to college in California and besides, we missed our friends there.

I told John I would only consider a coaching job on the West Coast.

A while later, John told me that Bethany College's athletic director and basketball coach, Phil Oates, was thinking of leaving, and wondered if I would be interested in the position.

Within a day or two, I got a call from the president of Bethany, Dick Foth. He asked if I would be interested in coming out to Bethany, and I said I was.

At the same time, Dick Gross, who had become a good friend, told me he was retiring as president of Gordon College. We had gone to many events together, played a lot of golf together, and joined in family gatherings. I knew without a doubt he had my back, or as the SEALS would say, he had my six.

Maybe it was time for me to leave.

I flew out to San Jose to visit Bethany College and met with Dick Foth, who offered me the job right away. After I returned home, Margie and I went to church, where the pastor's wife, Mona Johnian, was prophesying after her husband gave the message.

At the same time, I was praying for a clear message from the Lord about my future.

My head was bowed and my eyes were closed. As soon as I stopped praying, I looked up to see that Mona had stopped on her way to the stage, in the middle of the stairs. Our eyes locked. She looked at me, "The Lord has a word for you. Stand up," which I did.

At the end of her prophesizing, she said, "The Lord says, Go through the door I have opened for you, even though it will be very difficult."

Margie and I agreed that I would accept the Bethany job.

PART 21

Bethany College

CHAPTER 1

We were in some serious trouble

BY THE TIME WE WERE READY TO MOVE to Santa Cruz, we had given away all of our horses, except for our stallion and our best mare.

The mare was leased to a breeder where she was to be bred to a high-caliber stallion. The breeder would get the first foal and we would get the next one.

Margie and I decided to rent U-Hauls for our move to Santa Cruz. The large one carried all of our household furniture and clothing and towed a horse trailer with our stallion. Margie drove the smaller U-Haul, towing our car behind.

Allison, who was playing in an AAU volleyball tournament for the week in Florida, joined us later.

I drove with our two dogs, and Margie drove with Jeff and our two cats.

We planned on it being a four-day journey, but in the middle of the Ohio Turnpike, which is very up and down, the horse trailer buckled. Margie contacted me on our walkie-talkie — this was pre-cell phone — saying there were sparks flying from the trailer.

Thinking we were in some serious trouble, we both pulled off to the side. It was over 100 degrees and extremely humid.

After I saw that the trailer's hitch frame had collapsed, I remembered seeing a gas station about a mile back, so I started running in that direction.

Just as I approached the gas station, a man towing a stock trailer with landscaping equipment pulled in. After I told him my situation, he offered to help. He drove me back to where we had broken down and helped us load our stallion into his trailer.

Then we took the horse to a large farm belonging to one of his clients.

The owner had an empty barn and pastures and told me that I could leave the stallion there until I arranged to have it transported to Santa Cruz. He didn't charge me for boarding the stallion, even after it stayed there for two more months.

After we arranged for a tow truck to haul the trailer to a repair shop, we got back on the road again, this time with no trailer and no horse.

On our fourth day, we came to the Nevada-California border, where we were nervous at being inspected for plants. To make things worse, I had lost the key to the trailer. The inspector removed the lock with bolt cutters and when he looked inside, he saw nothing but cardboard boxes.

We sighed with relief as we drove into California.

After driving many hours, we began driving on Highway 17 into Santa Cruz late that night. Highway 17 is one of the most difficult and dangerous drives in California and Margie, who is the toughest woman I know, was exhausted and in tears. She said she couldn't go on, but somehow, we made it.

Mona's words that it would be difficult were beginning to prove prophetic, indeed. And we were just getting started.

Moving to Santa Cruz was made easier because of our longtime friends who lived there, Steve and Margie Haas, and Dan and Elaine Aldrich. We had all attended Hollywood Presbyterian Church together. Steve was the longtime track coach at San Jose City College, and Dan was the senior development associate at UC Santa Cruz.

We were very blessed to be immediately brought into their world of friends and fellowship.

This strengthened and created lifelong bonds that continue to this day.

PHOTO ALBUM 2

Los Raiders team photo from our second trip to Spain in 1980.

Teaching post-play positioning at a girls' club in Málaga, 2018.

Ruben Fernandez and I explaining to the congregation in Parque Victoria about our role in how their church came into existence.

Coaching this group in Málaga was a rewarding experience, especially after the parents gave me a standing ovation. When one mother asked why I did this for free, I told her that it was "a gift given to me that needs to be given away."

My first trip to Benin, relaxing in the President's airport lounge, with Romain Zannou (center) and Al Nordquist.

I'm with Aziz Adoumbou, at our first year of clinics for his youth basketball program in Benin.

The Gate of No Return in Ouidah, a symbol of the centuries-old curse. When slaves walked through the gate, the literal curse was that they'd never return to their African homeland, known as Dahomey.

The Tree of Forgetfulness, the actual tree in Ouidah where a curse was put upon slaves, forcing them to walk around the tree, seven times for males, nine times for females.

The Akpali village gathering that welcomed us upon our arrival.

A young girl with her friends, sitting at a desk in their Akpali school classroom.

With Al Nordquist and Steve Johnson, we're standing in front of the Portuguese Fort Museum in Ouidah.

Sitting with the young girl who was raised from the dead.

On my first trip Benin, I'm leading the cheer of "Benin!" with all the coaches. We did that at the end of every session.

Angeline, whom I helped to set up a seamstress business, with her children.

Along with a group connected to chicken farming in Ghana and the U.S., I'm meeting with President Kerekou (center, with sunglasses). There, I met Ron Weeks (far right) and we later formed an African non-profit called RedemptionWorks International.

In one of our ball-handling drills, this young baller looks like he's got it down.

Standing next to me, the village chief with the four young men that Romain sent to share the Word of Jesus with the village of Akpal.

We're In the home of François Tchokpodo (left), our driver, along with Archie Robinson.

My son Jeff in the village of Akpali. Notice how clean the village looks.

Reggie and Stacey Williams with the mother of the young girl (next to Stacey) who came back to life in Akpali. Stacey had a vision of the girl while worshipping in a church in Santa Barbara.

My son Jeff shooting an uncontested layup on the outdoor courts of the Olympic facility in Cotonou.

After losing a bet to the student life director at Bethany College, I had to perform a cheerleading routine at halftime at one of my games.

Circa 1970, I'm a cowboy on the open range of Sorrento Valley, where cattle were grazing and before there was the I-805 freeway.

At San Diego's Hall of Champions with (left to right) Monroe Nash and sports museum founder Bob Breitbard. We're holding one of Ted Williams' bats, which he gave to Breitbard, who was Williams' high school buddy and longtime friend.

After a doubles tennis match with NBA Hall of Famer George Yardley and his wife (at right), his two sons (at left), and his grandchildren. Also, there's former NBA player Keith Erickson (third from left), and NBA Hall of Famer Paul Westphal (fourth from left) and myself (next to Paul).

The Lord's Fitness and Community Development Center, at 43rd and Market streets.

With Terry Olsen, who led me to the Lord at Frontier Ranch many years ago, the summer before my senior year at Glendale High.

Together, we still have many trails ahead.

CHAPTER 2

'What are you doing here?'

As Bethany College's athletic director and basketball coach, I replaced Phil Oates, who became a very good friend.

Phil's dad, Buzz, was among the wealthiest people in the Sacramento Valley. He was also one of the most gracious people in using his wealth to further the kingdom of God, and Phil followed in his footsteps. Buzz was getting older and wanted Phil to come home and help him with the business.

Meanwhile, Allison started her senior year at Harbor High School, which had one of the most well-known volleyball programs in the CIF Northern California District. She adapted well to her new environment and her new team, which won the league title and went to the CIF Playoffs.

Later in the spring, the county held a televised award ceremony for the top athletes in various sports. We were at home sitting with Allison, watching it on TV, when the Athlete of the Year award was announced with a video introduction. We were shocked to see that the award winner was Allison Block.

All the other athletes were at the ceremony, receiving their awards, but there was Allison, sitting right next to us.

Both Margie and I looked at her and asked, "What're you doing here?"

She said she didn't care about awards. I understood because I had been the same way during my basketball career.

After graduating from high school, Allison went to UC Santa Barbara, where she played varsity volleyball. Her teammates knew that she was a very hard worker and probably the second-best athlete on the team, even as a freshman.

Early in her sophomore year I got a call from her. Her first words were, "Dad, I know you hate a quitter, but I can no longer play for Kathy."

Her coach, Kathy Gregory, was known as the toughest coach in the country and she'd been getting on Allison the whole season.

When I asked Allison what happened, she told me that during a practice Kathy was especially tough on her. According to Allison, Kathy had gone over the line by yelling at her, "Why can't you be as tough as your dad?"

I said I understood and asked her when she was going to tell Kathy of her decision.

She said, "Tomorrow at two o'clock." I told her I'd drive down the next morning to take her to lunch and pray for her while she was in the meeting.

After she quit the team, she felt an immense amount of relief and freedom.

CHAPTER 3

Laying out a fleece

THE PRESIDENT OF BETHANY COLLEGE, Dick Foth, was a very strong leader and a master communicator. He took me with him when he went to speak at different places and we developed a great relationship.

After I'd been there about a year, Dick resigned to be with and support his childhood friend John Ashcroft, who had just become Attorney General of the United States. Foth was connected with The Fellowship, a ministry led by Doug Coe in Washington D.C.

When Ashcroft came to visit Foth, they decided go fishing in Monterey Bay and rented a private fishing boat. They asked a couple of other friends and me to come along.

I knew that I usually get seasick, but for some reason I forgot to take Dramamine, a seasickness medicine.

Ashcroft was a sportsman and I really looked forward to spending some time with him. Instead, I spent my entire time leaning over the stern, regurgitating my breakfast.

Bethany's basketball team had suffered 19 straight years of losing records. They only had two sports — men's basketball and women's volleyball. One of the difficulties about taking over losing athletic programs is that some players have a hard time adjusting to a new coach, especially when that coach is me.

Phil Oates wanted to share his evaluation of his players, but I asked him not to do that because I wanted to evaluate them for myself.

Similar to my situation at UCSD and Gordon, I started off with 15 players and ended with eight. Those eight players were the foundation of the culture that I wanted to form. I knew from experience that these programs could be turned around quickly by recruiting players that were teachable, committed, and hard-working.

It also came back to the same old thing—I had to schedule wins.

When Dick Foth left Bethany after my first season, the school was overseen by the president of the faculty. At the end of my second season, I got a call from him saying they were eliminating the athletic program, which included my position. It seems they didn't think the athletic program was very important.

Despite that, they would continue paying my salary for the rest of the school year.

I was angry when I went home that night and prayed, "Lord, I'm bummed. What's happening with this whole thing?"

I had recruited six outstanding scholarship players. Continuing in my prayer, I said, "Lord, I know you want me to be here. I will work for free if five of those six players commit to play for me without getting scholarships."

Similar to what Gideon had done in the Old Testament, I was laying out a fleece of sorts. After praying, I called each player to explain the situation and asked if they would still play for me without a scholarship.

"Oh, by the way," I added, "I need your answer by noon tomorrow."

By noon the next day, five of the players called and said they would still come and play for me. I immediately called Phil Oates, told him the entire situation and that I could run the volleyball and the basketball program for $30,000 without me taking a salary.

When I asked if he would fund it, he said he would be glad to.

The administration agreed to keep the program going, knowing that it was funded. It was decided that we would run the program "off-book," meaning it was not officially part of the school system.

In spite of the circumstances, Margie and I agreed that I would continue at

Bethany. Margie, an occupational therapist, was working as an independent contractor, and she'd been able to double her work.

Because I didn't have a salary, I decided to activate my NBA retirement pension early, even though I knew that would cost me thousands of dollars in the long run.

Margie and I were renting a house that belonged to Bill Vickery, who was the Superintendent of the Northern California-Nevada district of the Assemblies of God and Chairman of the Board of Bethany College.

I had written the December rent check to him and got a note back from him saying he found out I was working for free.

He said I didn't have to pay rent for the next three months. Along with the note was my returned rent check.

The Lord was providing.

CHAPTER 4

It was a win-win

BETHANY SOON HIRED A NEW PRESIDENT, Tom Duncan, who had been an assistant to John Ashcroft when he was the governor of Missouri. Tom loved basketball.

Perfect, I thought.

After that first year of running the program off-book, Darrell Vaughn, who was a psychology professor at Bethany, and I connected. Darrell had just created a graduate program that he ran off-book. I met with him and he explained how he did it and that we should use it as a model for the athletic program.

We sat with Tom Duncan to explain how we could run an entrepreneurial athletic program off-book. We made a proposal to the administration that for every athlete we recruited and enrolled in Bethany, the school would get 33 percent of the tuition.

We would get the remaining 67 percent.

If we brought in enough new students, this new revenue source would pay my salary, the coach's salaries, the scholarships, and the budget for the entire athletic program. The school would also get room, board, and book fees.

It was a win-win with no risk for the college, so they voted yes. As Darrell and I left the meeting, we were ecstatic.

My goal was to bring as many student-athletes as possible to the school. We had only two sports, so I added women's basketball, softball, soccer, and we even made cheerleading a sport. The men's sports we added were soccer, baseball, and volleyball.

There were $500 scholarships available for every athlete enrolled, but for basketball there was more, because men's basketball was a flagship sport.

We hired part-time coaches that recruited extremely well and added 110 new student-athletes to a student body of around 600. There were more total students enrolled that year than in the school's long history. I also got local businesses to sponsor our program.

After two years of operating in the black, we were brought back on-book.

One day, I got a call from Al Nordquist's son, Chris, who was an assistant basketball coach at New Mexico State. He said he had a guard named Terry Bennett, one of the starters who had set an NCAA record for making nine straight 3-pointers in one game.

He was a tremendous player and an outstanding shooter. Through circumstances not under his control, he had to leave school. He was one of the five players that came to Bethany without a scholarship.

Terry enrolled in Bethany with only one year of playing eligibility, but he spent two years with me there, one as a player, and one as a graduate assistant coach. He was a great learner, and I could see that one day he'd be a great coach.

Later, he started a basketball program in Milwaukee called Athletes for Christ that produced some outstanding collegiate players.

One day, I was practicing what's called a "baseball passing drill," a conditioning drill. When I saw Terry squinting to see the ball that was passed to him, I asked him if his eyes were okay. I took him down to an optometrist to get checked, and we were told that he was legally blind.

Terry had been a prolific shooter and the doctor gave him a set of contact lenses, except that then he couldn't shoot the ball in the ocean. But after he took the contact lenses out and continued shooting simply by feel, he once again shot lights out.

Another one of those turnaround players was Joe Woods. Joe, who was married with children when he came to Bethany, was an outstanding athlete who became a very good basketball player. He was close friends with one of his teammates, Andre Huddleston.

In Andre's senior year, I was struggling with his attitude and his effect on the team. I talked with Joe about having Andre leave the team, but Joe became his advocate and told me it would destroy Andre if he couldn't play basketball his senior year.

Joe suggested that I tell Andre what I thought about his overall attitude and what he must do to stay on the team.

To inspire him, I said he was going to become the best defensive player in the league, and that I would have him guard our opponent's best players every game, no matter their size.

Because of his hard work, and that of our other players, Bethany had its best record in 21 years.

CHAPTER 5

With a handshake and a prayer

ONE YEAR, I WAS ASKED TO SPEAK TO Bethany's incoming freshman class at chapel. After I went to my office, a young man named Chris Blacksmith knocked on my door.

He told me he needed to be a part of a team because he felt he needed a support group during this significant transition in his life. He had come from a very difficult background and had recently become a believer in Jesus.

Problem was, he told me that he'd never been on a team and hadn't even played basketball.

Deeply moved by his story, I told him he could join the team and that practice started the next day. First, however, he had to cut his long blond hair, which would show me that he was really serious.

I talked to the team before practice and told them about Chris and that they needed to embrace him, have patience, and help teach him how to play. They all agreed.

Chris didn't play much until the last part of the season when I put him into a game, and he scored his first and only basket. The packed crowd gave him a standing ovation and his teammates and I went crazy.

After the season, Chris told me that being on the team was one of the greatest experiences of his life and that he didn't need to continue playing because he now had made lifelong friends.

Another memorable player was Clint Ladine, a point guard who came to

Bethany from Modesto Junior College. When I first saw him play, I knew immediately that I wanted him to play for me. He was smart, tough, hard-playing, and a leader.

He played for me for two years that were the two best years of Bethany basketball, where we beat D-2 Cal State LA, and the second-ranked D-2 team in the nation, Chapman College, coached by the legendary Bob Boyd.

Clint's life was radically changed by his coming to Bethany, hearing the gospel of Jesus, believing and receiving Jesus. He was dealing with a lot of issues, and just before he came to Bethany his parents had divorced.

He later married Marie France, one of my administrative assistants, who would sit in the gym and pray for the team.

After Clint graduated, my friend Al Nordquist helped him sign a pro contract to play basketball in Germany. Because his wife was French, he later signed a contract to play pro basketball in France.

When his career ended a few years later, he returned to work with his father-in-law, joining an inner-city ministry in the Tenderloin in San Francisco, which he later ran. He invited me to do a basketball clinic for the ministry a few blocks away from their headquarters, which I did.

I was really proud of what Clint was doing, and what he's gone on to accomplish.

About the same time, I was made aware of a high school player in Sacramento from a small Christian school, Kirk Smith, whose father had played basketball at Bethany.

Raised as a missionary's kid in Ecuador, amazingly he had attended the same school in Quito where my son and daughter-in-law would later teach as missionaries.

After I saw him play, Kirk told me he wanted to play for me at Bethany, but I told him that it would be very difficult. We had a very good team, and I knew it would take some time for him to accomplish his goal. I knew that I could make him a better player and told him I was willing to give him an opportunity.

We made an agreement that I would teach him as long as he was patient and worked hard. We sealed our agreement with a handshake and a prayer.

His freshman year, I pushed him hard to learn how to fundamentally play the game of basketball with focus, intensity and heart. I pushed him hard to excel to the point where the other players were questioning why I was pushing him so hard.

He played very little his freshman year and came to me after the season to say he was thinking about quitting, that it wasn't worth all the hard work and pressure. I told him we had made an agreement, which was for him to keep working hard to become a good, competitive basketball player.

The next season was much the same. I encouraged him to keep working hard. Still, he didn't play very much that year. He came to me again, questioning if it was all worth it and that he was thinking about quitting. I wouldn't let him.

His junior year was the same — hard work, but not playing much. He came to me again, but based on our agreement, I wouldn't let him quit.

During his senior year, he became a tough fundamental, competitive basketball player. He was not a starter, but he was a big contributor to a very successful team. I was very proud of Kirk when he graduated and got married to a girl from Bethany College.

Kirk later became a professional comedian and wrote a book about his autistic son. In the book, he mentioned that I had helped prepare him for some of the challenges he would face in life.

CHAPTER 6

With conviction and passion

At Santa Cruz High, the basketball coach, Pete Newell Jr., was excited to have our son Jeff on the team because he was my son and had the potential to be as tall as I was.

Pete put him on the varsity, even though I thought he should be on junior varsity. Jeff was also in a youth band as a bass guitar player, and he loved to write poetry and songs.

A few days before basketball season began, his senior year, Jeff came home after school and asked if he could talk to me. He asked me what I would think if he didn't play basketball his senior year.

I asked him what his passion was, even though I already knew the answer. It was obvious. He didn't practice basketball on our driveway, but was in his room practicing his guitar and writing. Still, I wanted him to tell me himself. He told me he loved music and writing.

I affirmed to him that he didn't need to play basketball, and that whatever he did, to do it with conviction and passion. He was relieved and asked if Mom would be okay with his decision. I said, I don't think so, but that I would take care of it.

Not long afterward, Jeff became a staff writer on the school newspaper, which was distributed throughout Santa Cruz.

One day, I got a call from a friend saying she had read Jeff's column and that it brought her to tears. The column was titled "Great Expectations," and subtitled "Thoughts About Life, Basketball, and My Dad."

It brought tears to my eyes, too.

CHAPTER 7

So obnoxious and opinionated

AFTER BEING ON CHRISTIAN CAMPUSES full-time, I sometimes desired to be around more non-Christians. At Bethany, I prayed, "Lord, bring someone new into my life."

Shortly afterward, I was having lunch in the Bethany dining room where I joined a group of women having lunch. They were all wonderful people, and we all lived in the same neighborhood.

One of them asked, "Have you seen this guy walking with this little dog? He's pretty scary-looking, all tatted up with long gray hair and a big, gray beard."

I listened and then replied that I'd never seen anyone who matched that description.

The next morning, I went out to get the newspaper and there was a man with long gray hair and a big, gray beard, standing right in front of the house with his little dog. Although he looked much older, it turned out that he was a year younger than me.

When I asked him, "Hey, how're you doing?" he replied, "Not very good. My wife left me yesterday."

I said, "My name's John Block," and he said, "My name is Robert Reader. I know who you are. I knew who you were when you were at Gordon College. I knew you were coming to Bethany, because I'd been living just down the road, in Salem before my wife and I decided we'd move back to Santa Cruz."

He was also familiar with my NBA career.

I said, "It was good meeting you, Robert," before returning to the house. As it turned out, he lived only two doors down from us.

That day I decided not to eat in the dining room, but to go home for lunch. I was driving the two blocks back from Bethany to home and there he was — sitting on a step outside a garage with a book in his hand. I stopped in the middle of the street and asked what he was doing.

He said, "I'm trying to read this book."

I invited him to watch our practice that day and he showed up with his little dog, Tinker. I told the team about him and that I wanted them to embrace and pray for him. For the rest of the season, he didn't miss a practice.

One time when we were in the middle of a drill, Tinker scampered onto the court.

We all loved it.

It turned out that Robert had been a biker who hung around with the Hell's Angels. He told me he had done drugs and been an alcoholic since his teens, but had stopped all substance abuse about ten years earlier.

He was easily the most obnoxious person I had ever met in my life — he appeared to hate women and was unbelievably opinionated. I could really understand why his wife left him. I would take him to church and afterward he would argue about everything he heard.

At times, I would have him come back to my home and my wife and daughter would have to leave because he was so obnoxious and opinionated.

In response, I would talk to him about Jesus. Robert became a big part of the team, and I invited him to travel with us. Meanwhile, we were all praying for him.

Through my connection with the Sacramento Kings, I was able to convince them to allow our team to play a game before their NBA game. This was just not done, but the Kings agreed. The game was between Bethany and Biola University, my longtime nemesis.

Robert was seated on the bench when I asked him to bring the water jug into the locker room at halftime. He lifted it by the lid and water spilled all over the floor. He was really upset and embarrassed, but we told him that everything was okay, and that the maintenance crew would clean it up.

We were all learning about the grace of God.

As for the game itself, despite being huge underdogs, we won.

CHAPTER 8

This was unheard of

AFTER ROBERT'S WIFE LEFT HIM, he fell behind on his rent and his landlord was ready to boot him out. I convinced his landlord to be patient and I paid for some of his rent on occasion. The local market gave me food to give to him.

Later, I helped him land a job doing food preparation at a restaurant, but he hated it and quit after a week. Too much pressure. When I found out he had driven 18-wheelers, I helped him get a delivery job, which he totally enjoyed.

One day, he arrived in the middle of practice, and he had a short haircut and had shaved his beard. Everybody on the team stopped practicing and started clapping for Robert.

After he got a job, I suggested that he start sending his wife a monthly check. He said she wouldn't respond, but he ended up writing her anyway and sent her a check for ten bucks.

He showed me the letter he received back from her and it was addressed to their dog. It said, "Dear Tinker, would you tell Robert that I don't need any money." Robert was totally bummed and said, "Look, she even wrote the letter to Tinker."

I said, "At least she wrote you back. It was really addressed to you."

I suggested that he should continue to write her, along with sending a check every month.

After some time, Robert told me he had received Jesus. He had approached a well-known pastor, Chip Ingram of Santa Cruz Bible Church, and asked Chip if I could baptize Robert in one of the services. This was unheard of, that a layman would baptize someone in that church, but Chip agreed, and I baptized Robert.

Margie and I had decided to take a family camping trip around the country that summer. We left from Santa Cruz and traveled to 10 national parks, starting with Yellowstone and continuing a Northern route across the U.S., through South Dakota to see Mt. Rushmore and on to Niagara Falls before finally arriving in Boston.

There, I got in touch with Robert's wife, and we agreed to meet in a McDonald's parking lot. She said Robert had a way of manipulating people and that he had even manipulated me into talking to her.

I told her that I understood, but wanted to express how much Robert had changed, that he now knew the Lord Jesus and wanted her to come back to him.

Still, she insisted that there was no way that would happen.

When we got back to Santa Cruz, I saw Robert and he asked what I had said to his wife. He said he had just received her divorce papers, but that she hadn't signed them. I suggested that he should keep writing her and sending her money. Not too much later, she decided to rejoin him in Santa Cruz.

They were together until Robert passed away in 2021.

CHAPTER 9

From junkyard to dream home

WHILE WE WERE LIVING NEAR BETHANY, we had boarded our stallion, Sultan Sayid, on a friend's property near Henry Cowell Park.

This was a very desirable neighborhood in which to live. Every time Margie rode, she passed these beautiful homes — except for one particular home that was literally a junk heap.

The front yard was filled with old boats and about a dozen junky cars. Every time Margie rode by this house, she would pray that we could buy it. In a way, it was like she was walking around the walls of Jericho.

It did come on the market, and the real estate agent lived just a couple blocks from us.

There were two conditions to see the property. One was that a sheriff had to be there to restrain the owner's son, who in the past had been abusive and threatened potential buyers. The other was that we had only ten minutes to view the property.

What we saw both inside and outside the house was appalling.

There was trash everywhere, and a large fireplace where they had burned their trash. The entire fireplace and the wall were caked in soot. There must have been a thousand auto parts strewn over the floor in the master bedroom.

The backyard was covered in junk and lumber. The swimming pool, which looked like it hadn't been used for many years, had over 30 tires in it.

But it was perfect for us and we told the realtor that we wanted to buy it.

After that not-so-great viewing, the realtor expressed to us that he would work hard to get this house for us. The problem was, there were already two offers in.

He suggested we put our offer in and said that if we were patient, he thought we would get the house. He didn't believe that the other offers would hold.

Three months later, our offer was accepted. It took two more months for the seller to clear everything out. Then it took months of work just to make the house livable enough for us to move in. Whenever friends came by, they were in shock.

What, you bought this house?

Margie is a master visionary on what can be done to a home. We proceeded to transform the house and property from a junkyard to our dream home.

Now Margie could walk to our horse, which we stabled at a good friend's property. From there, she rode among the many trails of nearby 4,600-acre Henry Cowell Redwood State Park.

Glorious.

PART 22

A family adventure

CHAPTER 1

'Turn back now!'

WHEN OUR CAMPING TRIP TOOK US to the Grand Canyon, we camped on the north rim, which is about 3,000 feet higher than the south rim. Allison, who thoroughly researches everything, found that the North Kaibab Trail near our campground went down to the Colorado River.

She wanted to hike with Jeff down to the river on this trail. She said it shouldn't be any problem, that it was "just" a 27-mile round trip. At 6 in the morning, I dropped them off at the trailhead with some sandwiches and water. Margie agreed to hike with me down the trail for two miles.

We started at 10 that morning and got down about half a mile when we ran into a German couple that were on their way back up. We asked them how the trail was. After looking at us, they emphatically said, "Turn back now!"

We did not heed their advice.

The route was so steep and narrow that it took us a total of three hours just to hike down two miles. We were both exhausted and dreaded going back up. The return trip took six hours, and by then it was nearly dark. We immediately went to the ranger station to tell them about our kids who were hiking the entire trail in one day.

He told us that even the most experienced hikers don't do that. Then he called a campground down the trail to see if they had seen our kids. The ranger said they had left there, and were on their way back up the trail. He recommended that I go to the trailhead and wait for them.

He figured they might arrive between midnight and 1 in the morning.

I have never prayed so hard and so long. I knew how dangerous the trail was even during the daytime. I also knew that Allison and Jeff only had windbreakers and the temperature there would drop 30 to 40 degrees at night.

Finally, at 1 in the morning, they came up the trail, spotted me there and began yelling with excitement and joy. We returned to our campsite and Margie fixed dinner for all of us while we heard their story. They had made it to the river easily, but it was very difficult coming back.

They had eaten their sandwiches and were doing fine until they got near the area where Margie and I had turned around.

The moon was not up yet and when their flashlight battery died, it was basically pitch black. The way they handled it was to hug each other going up the trail with one of them touching the side of the slope of the trail, so they wouldn't fall down a 2,000-foot drop off.

They got so tired that they laid down on the trail, wanting to go to sleep, but Allison said they had to keep going because Mom was going to be really worried.

Sitting at that table with all of us exhausted, we looked at each other and, nearly in unison said, "This trip is over, let's go home."

We had driven 9,000 miles in 35 days.

PART 23

Bethany to PLNU

CHAPTER 1

They stopped it cold

BETHANY PRESIDENT TOM DUNCAN and I shared an ambitious vision of what the college could become.

My friend Buzz Oates, Phil Oates' father who had given many properties to churches over the year, wanted Bethany to relocate to a site near Sacramento. He had in mind a 50-acre parcel that he owned not far from Folsom.

Tom and I visited and walked the property, which was located amid many oak trees and near a small town, and we agreed it would be a perfect place for a college campus.

Buzz told us he was willing to build the campus for us. Tom and I started planning with Buzz and Phil about how to make the transition. Buzz owned a resort hotel with a pool, tennis courts and housing for a few hundred guests.

The big question was, without existing facilities, where would we run our athletic program? To make it work, I knew we'd have to use other schools' facilities, at least temporarily.

But, when we presented the idea to Bethany's board, they stopped it cold. The major reason was that the hotel was located in West Sacramento, a run-down part of town at the time. They didn't want female students in such a bad area, even though the hotel itself was nice enough.

By the way, I don't think they had a clue about the neighborhood that surrounded USC when I was going there.

Precisely because of its location, both Tom and I believed there was no better place for a Christian campus. We believed we could bring the light of the gospel to a dark place.

Not much later, in my sixth year at Bethany College, Tom met with me and said, "John, I'm leaving, and I recommend that you leave, too."

Within about a week of talking with Tom about leaving Bethany, I got a call from Jim Bond, the president of Point Loma Nazarene University (PLNU) in San Diego.

Jim had been a tremendous basketball player at Pasadena Nazarene College and was a very effective leader. He said, "I understand you may be looking to make a move."

I said that I was, and he said, "We've had 15 years of losing records in our basketball program and we want you to come and turn it around."

I was hired and my contract started in June of 1997.

CHAPTER 2

We had made lifelong friends

PROVERBS 16:9 SAYS, *"A man's heart plans his way, but the Lord directs his steps."*

That has been true and continues to be true in my life. My lifelong friend, Bill Westphal, with whom I had remained in touch over the years, was struggling after losing his high school position in Phoenix.

I asked him to be my assistant coach at PLNU and he agreed. He was also hired to be a professor in the Physical Education department.

The Santa Cruz home had been our dream home. We had made lifelong friends, and our horses were boarded just a few blocks away with 150 miles of pristine riding trails within blocks. The house with its pool was perfect for us.

Margie didn't want to move or sell our house, but she knew we had to. For a while I drove back and forth between San Diego and Santa Cruz, but that ended on August 1 when I needed to be on campus full-time.

On a Friday, Margie put a small "for sale" sign behind a knoll on the main road. On Saturday morning, she called me to say we had six offers, all over our asking price, and that I needed to fly up there. After selling the house, we moved into married student housing on the PLNU campus.

This was our 35th move, and the plants we had been hauling all around the country we now moved into a garage below us. Bill and Lynne Westphal also moved into married-student housing.

On our first Sunday together in San Diego, Margie and I visited Coast

Vineyard, the church Don Williams was pastoring in La Jolla. After the service, Don made a point of introducing us to Jim and Sandi Green. Jim had been a Young Life leader and was now involved in developing the Naval Training Center in Point Loma.

Within a week, we were meeting with a good friend of Jim's, Milt Richards, who had just moved to San Diego with his family from Camarillo.

Together, Jim, Milt, and I decided immediately to start a men's group that would meet at the Naval Training Center. That group would become the foundational support for one of the most difficult times in my life.

CHAPTER 3

'I'm in a win-win situation'

THERE WERE VERY FEW PLAYERS RETURNING to PLNU and I had to scramble to put together a team. I brought some players in, but some of them didn't fit into PLNU.

One of the players who did fit was Archie Ray Robinson, a point guard from San Diego City College. While Archie Ray took a walk around the campus, I was sitting in my office with his dad, Pastor Archie Robinson, who asked me, "If my son comes here, will you love him?" No parent had ever asked me that before.

"Yes, I will," I replied.

That season I had three different teams — the team I started with, the team I had during semester break, and the team after the break. Some players were asked to leave the school, and other players quit, so I had to get intramural players to fill their spots by the second semester.

Sadly, Archie Ray became ineligible to play because of a glitch in the transfer of units from his junior college.

I had been in some bad situations as a coach, but that first year at Point Loma was the worst ever. On a Friday toward the end of the season, I went in for a stress EKG test. I was on a treadmill, and they pulled me off after six minutes.

The surgeon asked me if I was under any stress. I told him I was a college basketball coach and that my team was 2–22. He said, "Your test doesn't look good. We've scheduled an angiogram Monday to check out what's going on."

On Saturday, I was scheduled to travel to Santa Barbara by bus with my team to play Westmont College. Jeff Reinke called me just before I was walking out the door to go to the bus. He asked how I was doing, and I told him about the stress test and the scheduled angiogram.

He said he'd pray for me.

Not two minutes later as I was leaving, he called me back and told me that I shouldn't travel with the team. I knew this was God's way of telling me to stay home. I went to the bus and told the assistant coach I wasn't going on the trip.

On Monday, after the angiogram the doctor said I had 95 percent blockages in three of my arteries and 90 percent in the other. He said he couldn't understand why I hadn't already had a heart attack. He also told me they were immediately taking me in for a quadruple bypass open-heart surgery.

Margie, Allison, and Jeff were outside in the hallway as I was being wheeled into the operating room. They were in tears. It was a very emotional time as they prayed for me, and I prayed for them.

As I was moved through the doors of the operating room, I had a conversation with the Lord, saying, "Lord, I'm in a win-win situation, I'm going into this surgery praising and worshiping you for the life you've given me.

"If I make it out of here, I'll be praising and worshiping you for the life you've given me. If I don't, I'll be in your presence praising and worshiping you."

At that very moment, all fear of death left me. It hasn't been a part of my life since.

Instead of being a three-and-a-half-hour surgery, it took seven hours. When I awoke, I had a tremendous reaction to the anesthesia and began vomiting uncontrollably. I was in the hospital longer than normal before returning home to our two-bedroom campus apartment.

On the first night home, I took Vicodin for the pain and it led to night terrors. I woke up and asked Margie to pray for me. After that, I never took Vicodin or any other narcotic painkillers again.

CHAPTER 4

A strong relationship was forged

THE REHAB AND RECOVERY WERE VERY SLOW and it took an entire year before I was fully recovered. When I coached that next season, the lingering effects of the operation created a brain fog where I was not as sharp as I needed to be.

Through my recovery and beyond, PNLU's chief financial officer, Art Shingler, and I connected through his love of basketball. He had played for Pasadena Nazarene College before I played at USC, and had undergone open-heart, nine-bypass surgery just before mine.

We encouraged each other through our rehabs, and a strong relationship was forged between us that has lasted ever since.

That spring, Darnell Cherry walked into my office. He was a 6-11 basketball player who had played in junior college in San Diego before transferring to Manhattan College in New York City. He told me that he had gotten into "the New York scene" and lost his scholarship, but he'd also heard that I gave players second chances.

I really liked his humble attitude and that he said he'd do anything to get accepted by PLNU and play for me.

As I often did with other players, the test was to see how quickly he would get his transcripts to admissions. He got the official transcripts sent within a couple days. His grades were appalling.

His overall GPA was 1.2, and in his last semester he had only completed three units. He needed a total of 24 units and an overall GPA of 2.0 to be eligible to play at PLNU. To accomplish this, he would need 21 units with a 3.8 GPA, to be completed by the first day of classes.

I knew he had a possibility of accomplishing this at National University, where he could take four classes per month.

Darnell and I met with a good counselor at National and we told her the situation. She came up with a plan for him to get the required units by August. On August 1, we got his transcripts from National to be evaluated. His overall GPA was now 1.9.

He said, "Now what do I do?" I told him I'd figure something out. Admissions told me he needed two more classes and that they had to be A's.

I requested they give Darnell a provisional admission, so he could start full-time classes while taking the two classes at National.

His desire and dedication to attend PLNU and play for me was rewarded. He got his two A's.

After that year, I made him a graduate assistant coach, so I could scholarship him and he could graduate. He went on to get his master's degree at National University.

Meanwhile, Art Shingler had put together a program for the school to invest money to help faculty and staff purchase houses in the area. They would help with our down payment, and they would then own a percentage of the house. Both Bill Westphal and I bought houses close to the school.

Within two years, the value of our homes skyrocketed, and interest rates dropped. So, we refinanced and I was able to pay back PLNU's ownership percentage.

Happily, Margie and I still live there.

CHAPTER 5

Ashamed of their complaints

THE YEAR BEFORE WE HAD WON EIGHT GAMES, and that year we won 15, in large part because of Darnell and his buddy, Simon Phipps, our outstanding point guard.

For me, the highlight of the season was when we went into the league tournament as the eighth seed, playing against the first seed, Azusa Pacific, at their home. They were perennial winners of the league, and we beat them in overtime.

It was like we had won a championship.

During that season, I met with PLNU's director of missions and said I wanted to take my team overseas on a short-term mission trip. Not long after, he called to say he had a place for us to go — Palestine.

When my family found out about the trip, Allison suggested we spend an extra week in Israel and Jordan. She put together the whole itinerary, and would also served our family as tour guide. Early in the summer we took some of the players on my team and my family to Palestine and Israel.

The first week our family and the team stayed in Ramallah at the Ramallah Hotel, a mere two blocks from Yasser Arafat's compound.

We played a basketball game in Ramallah and did a clinic. We also played games all over the West Bank. One of the most memorable places was in Gaza City, where the women in our group were not allowed to go because it was considered too dangerous for them.

After a long drive, we left our van outside Israeli border security. From there we traveled in a school bus. The players complained about being hungry, wondering when they would be able to eat.

When we entered the largest refugee camp in the world, the driver, who had grown up in that camp, pointed to his left where there were acres and acres of garbage and trash.

When we all saw dogs and children rummaging through the garbage for scraps of food, the players were in shock and then ashamed of their complaints. We held our clinic in Gaza City with many Palestinian children participating and a large crowd of spectators looking on.

One of the guests at the Ramallah Hotel recognized me from my days of playing at USC. Through the hotel owner, a meeting was arranged with the head of the Egyptian Agricultural Organization. He was with two men of the same position, one from Lebanon, the other from Syria.

He told me that he had seen all of my games in college when USC visited Cal Berkeley, which he had attended. He asked if his two colleagues could join us, and I said yes. When they did, we discussed my impressions of Palestine, which affirmed their frustration.

They had been there a week to meet with Palestinian leaders to guide them into building an agricultural organization so the Palestinians could become more self-sufficient. They found it difficult because there was no central leadership.

When nothing was accomplished, they left, very discouraged.

After our games and clinics, there was a tour guide provided for us to tour Jerusalem. Two of the major highlights from that time were walking the Hezekiah Tunnel, which was built thousands of years ago out of solid rock by King Hezekiah.

More than 580 yards long, it travels from the Pool of Siloam into Jerusalem. Built in two directions that miraculously meet in the middle, the tunnel was so dark that we had to walk with candles because flashlights were forbidden.

Though I had to walk hunched over at the waist the entire way, it was an experience that we'll never forget.

Later, we got connected with an Arab Palestinian Nazarene pastor named Nabil. We were given the opportunity to go to the Jordan River where Nabil would baptize anyone who wanted to be baptized. Some members of the team, along with Margie and our son Jeff, were baptized.

The PLNU team traveled back to the U.S. and our family stayed for another week. We spent our first night in a Nazarene church in Bethlehem, where Nabil was one of the pastors. We were hosted by one of the other pastors who was from England.

We woke up early to get on the road, and when we went downstairs to the kitchen and dining room area, everything was set up for our breakfast.

The pastor and his wife had been cooking and we thanked them, but said we were ready to leave. He replied, "Are we pagans that we can't eat and pray together?"

We stayed for breakfast, which was delicious.

CHAPTER 6

We had to get back to the border

ANOTHER HIGHLIGHT WAS WHEN Nabil invited us to have dinner with his family. The house was four stories tall, and the top story was unfinished. As the family clan grew, more levels would be added.

Nabil brought us into a big room with numerous couches lining it. There was a huge dining room with a huge kitchen. When we got there, all of the family members, including Nabil's parents, his siblings and their children were there. Nabil was the only one in the family who spoke English.

The family expressed great appreciation that we were there and honored us.

When we were called to dinner, Nabil told us that his mother had put together a traditional Palestinian dinner that was heart healthy, because they knew that I had undergone heart surgery only a year before.

We traveled all over Israel seeing all the major sites. Toward the end of our trip, we visited the ancient city of Petra, in Jordan, which was built out of solid rock. One problem was that Margie had been very sick with strep throat and 102-plus fever.

She was on antibiotics, but didn't stay on them long enough.

At the border of Jordan, they did not allow us to take our rental car into the country. We had to take a taxi to a town near Petra. We arrived in the evening and spent the night in the Cleopetra Hotel, which seemed to be designed for very small people.

We were told that it takes two days to tour Petra, which we couldn't do because we had to get back to the border before dark. We hiked around Petra in 100-degree temperatures with Margie's temperature spiking.

She was really struggling as we climbed all over Petra. We were climbing up to one site where Margie didn't think she could make it. I told her they had a Coke vendor at the top, so she kept climbing. She really is tough.

It was getting late when we got a taxi and we told the driver we had to get to the border before it closed. He was screaming down this shortcut on an unfinished dirt highway that he wasn't supposed to be driving on. We made it in time.

Petra is one of the most amazing sites we've ever seen.

CHAPTER 7

The rock of the team

PLNU WENT 28–7 IN MY THIRD SEASON, which was the best they had done in years. The year before we were 15–17.

The major reasons for our success were the addition of a new assistant coach, Bruce Schooling, and one very impactful player, Willie Brisco.

Schooling also served as a professor in PLNU's business department and would soon become the school's professor of the year and the head of his department. One time he spoke at chapel, where I was working.

I enjoyed Schooling's presentation so much that I wanted to get to know him. As soon as chapel was over, I introduced myself and we ended up spending time together as friends. The next year he became a volunteer assistant coach, something he did for two years.

Through all my years of coaching, Biola always had great teams and was almost always ranked nationally. Dave Holmquist had been their coach all those years.

While I was the athletic director and basketball coach at Gordon, Dave visited me to find out what it was like holding both roles, because Biola also wanted him to be athletic director. I gave him my thoughts, and he ended up taking the position.

Josh Williams was a 5-8 high school point guard from Bakersfield, who wanted to come to PLNU directly out of high school. However, I suggested that he instead go to Bakersfield Community College (BCC) to gain more experience. That proved to be one of the biggest coaching mistakes I ever made.

Josh led BCC to the California Community College championship game. I watched him outplay two of the best athletes on the opposing team. They were taller, jumped higher, were faster and quicker, but he handled them.

After Josh's freshman season, he and his dad, Duane, who was a captain in the Bakersfield fire department, came to PLNU for an official campus visit to discuss the possibilities of a basketball scholarship. While Josh toured the campus, Duane and I met in my office.

He said, "If you don't love Josh once his college career is over, I will repay back the full amount of the scholarship." Much like Pastor Archie Robinson asking me if I was going to love his son, this was one of the most remarkable things a parent has ever said to me.

When Josh graduated, his dad was right. I loved this kid, and he was one of the most impressive players I've ever coached.

Willie Brisco had played two years of community college basketball in Portland, but hadn't played for ten years. At 30, he was an imposing 6-6 athlete, very wise in both life and basketball.

Because he was much older than his teammates, he proved to be the rock of the team. He was a mentor and like an assistant coach to the other players.

Just like Darnell Cherry, after playing for me for two years, Willie became my graduate assistant with a scholarship so he could graduate. He later founded a significant and impactful charity, Hope Leadership, which works with youth.

I first heard of Travis Lindstrom when I got a call from his coach at University of Hawaii-Hilo. I had never heard a coach speak so highly of a player and how he could impact a team — and win.

Travis was a very smart player and a fierce competitor. Plus, his father was a highly successful basketball coach in the Pacific Northwest.

I would set up competitive practice drills and Travis never lost once. He shot 90 percent for the season from the free-throw line and during the last five minutes of a game, he never missed a single free-throw. If we were ahead with five minutes to go, we never lost.

Travis ended up playing pro basketball in Australia, where he met his wife and continues to live.

CHAPTER 8

'We have a big problem here'

ONE OF THE MAJOR HIGHLIGHTS of the 1999–2000 season was beating Biola twice in league and again in the conference tournament. To defeat that good a team three straight times is very, very difficult.

Tyler Miller, who was involved with me at the founding of Oakbridge, invited Margie and me to attend a small weekend seminar led by nationally famed author Os Guinness.

During the introductions, the co-leader of the seminar, Michael Cromartie, who was known as "the Christian media ambassador to Washington D.C.," was amazed to see me there.

He said that he was one of the Young Life high school kids who had attended the Atlanta Hawks game with tickets I had given to Mal McSwain, his Young Life leader. Michael said that he would never forget going to that game and going to dinner with us afterwards where we talked about our relationship with Jesus.

While my fourth season at PLNU was a disappointment, one highlight for me was meeting the commander of the Navy SEALs, who was a believer in Jesus. I had him speak to my team one day, and he gave us some of the core values of being a team.

The most important thing for a SEAL, he told us, was the mission. The next most important thing was protecting your buddy. The last was staying alive. He asked our team what the most dangerous thing was for a SEAL. There were all sorts of answers like sharks, enemy fire, and drowning.

He said no, the most dangerous thing for a SEAL was a bad buddy. About a week later we went to the SEAL training center in Coronado, where he put the team through some competitive games to highlight what he had just taught us.

I invited Alex Hannum, my former coach with the San Diego Rockets, to observe my team as they went through their competitive drills. The team got to experience me honoring him, which was the last time I saw him before he passed away.

Looking back, my time at PLNU was challenging in many ways. One was that I had five surgeries, two of which were major. The other challenge was with the two administrators who were overseeing me.

Let's just say that there were differences in our philosophies.

It all came to a head after my fourth season when I was asked to meet with the school's president, along with the student life director and the athletic director.

The night before the meeting, during a conversation with Art Schingler, he advised me to not react defensively, not to take offense, and to calmly answer any accusations against me.

I wanted Bruce Schooling to be my advocate at the meeting, and they said that would be fine. In the meeting, they handed me three pages of accusations, and I calmly went through each item for about two hours.

By the time I finished, the president looked to the athletic director and said, "I think we have a big problem here. It seems like you guys need to work this out."

Bruce, who hadn't said a word, asked if he could speak. He said his daughter was a basketball player who wanted to be a coach, and that he'd be proud to have John Block serve as her coach and teach her how to be a coach.

His remarks were greeted with silence.

When I left the room, the athletic director asked if he could walk with me back to the gym. He said he had made a mistake in compiling his list. He offered his apology and his hope that we could work things out.

CHAPTER 9

I needed to get out of coaching

IMMEDIATELY AFTER THAT, I made a commitment to the Lord that I would never again get offended by anyone.

I knew I would need His strength and power to not get offended — not with the people who wanted to fire me, not with the person who cut me off on the highway, not with my wife, not with anybody.

If the Christ who lives in me did not take offense when he was reviled and people said all manner of evil things about him, then beat him and crucified him, I'm not going to take offense either.

That commitment stands to this day.

Through all the challenges, turmoil and physical problems I was having, I continued getting great support from the group of friends whom I had met with every Thursday during my tenure at PLNU.

At the beginning of my last year there, we were meeting for breakfast when one of the fellas said that I needed to get out of coaching. He said, "We'll even write your resignation letter." I said, "No, I'm not resigning."

They all agreed that I was very stubborn. I explained to them that during my professional career I had never pursued any position by myself because I believed that it was God who directed my path. God put me into positions and God would take me out. It's His timing, not my own.

Our team was in the midst of a horrendous year. I had made a mistake in bringing in too many young players, many of whom were not able to handle my coaching style.

Toward the end of January, things continued to get worse. I was called into a meeting with the athletic director and the student life director. They said they were making a change and that they had decided to let me go. They offered me two severance packages.

One was if I resigned, and the other was if I was fired.

I asked them, "What is the truth?" They answered, "We're firing you." I said, "That's the package I'm going to take." They told me that I could not go back to my office in the gym to get my personal effects until the weekend.

As I left the meeting to walk home, only three blocks away, I thought, well, Lord, what do you have for me now?

Little did I know what the answer to that prayer would be.

PART 24

Benin

CHAPTER 1

Minutes after I'd been fired

I COULDN'T CALL MY WIFE TO TELL HER what had happened because she was at work. As soon as I got home, I called my friend Milt Richards to tell him what had happened.

He was in Arlington, Virginia, meeting with Doug Coe, the overseer of The Fellowship, which coordinates Congress' annual National Prayer Breakfast.

At the exact time I called Milt, Doug Coe also took a call. Milt stepped out of the room, and I told him I had been fired. He said, "At the risk of sounding insensitive, Praise God!" We talked and laughed a bit longer before ending the call.

As Milt went back into the room, Doug was just hanging up from his call and he asked Milt, "What's your coaching friend doing now?" Milt said, "That was him on the phone. He just got fired. He's now available."

Doug said, "Well, that's amazing because that was Mathieu Kerekou, the President of Benin, Africa. He was asking me if I knew of a college basketball coach who had played in the NBA, loves the Lord and can come help build a basketball program for his country in the name of Jesus."

That was only minutes after I'd been fired. A few minutes ago, I was the basketball coach of a small college, and now I was going to help build a basketball program for a small African nation.

Milt Richards, who was from Adelaide, Australia, and I were developing a strong relationship. Though he had a robust waistline, he was still a very good athlete who had played Australian Rules Football professionally, and was a good tennis player and golfer. We played doubles tennis and many rounds of golf together.

He was very connected to The Fellowship, an international ministry of relationships of religious, business, and political leaders, based on the teachings of Jesus. Internationally, small groups of men meet with the purpose of sharing their lives and encouraging each other through the teachings of Jesus.

Influential people from around the world gather there to build unity around Jesus. This is the world that Milt and Doug Coe brought me into.

Within weeks of my call to Milt, I received an official letter from the president of Benin, inviting me to his country. I got in touch with Al Nordquist, my covenant brother. I asked him if he wanted to go to Benin with me and my son Jeff, and without any hesitation, he said yes.

A three-week trip was planned for June without us knowing what we were going to do or how we were going to do it.

Doug Coe wanted us to be under the covering of Oklahoma U.S. Senator James Inhofe. Senator Inhofe was deeply and passionately involved with Africa, specifically Benin, as well as with the country's top leader, President Kerekou.

The plan was that after we completed our trip to Benin we would come back through Washington D.C., and give Senator Inhofe a report on our experience.

We always want to know who we were coaching, how many, when, and where. We like as much information as possible so that we can prepare to teach and be organized.

We agreed to go with no set agenda and no expectations, which was unusual for us. We knew we were going there to serve Benin and its president. And the Lord.

CHAPTER 2

He had been a dictator

En route to Benin, on our connecting flight to London, Al, my son Jeff and I all sat in economy, which has never been comfortable for my 6-9 frame.

I had the worst seat possible — an aisle seat in the back near the restrooms where people were banging into me all night long. After flying in from London, we arrived in Benin during the day after 36 hours of travel.

The airport was small, and after walking down a stairway onto the tarmac, we were met by a searing wall of tropical heat. We were escorted to the President's lounge, where we met our host, Romain Zannou.

Benin had been a French colony and most of its people spoke French. Romain was fluent in English, French and many other African dialects. While we waited for our luggage to arrive and our passports to be processed, I told Romain that we had come to serve him, the President, and the people of Benin.

When I said that, he looked at me and said, "John, you are the first Westerner who has ever come here and said that to us. Most everyone who comes here has their own agenda."

As we found out later, Romain had led President Kerekou to the Lord. He was the head of the Four Square Church in Benin, and one of the most gifted men I have ever known. From his communication with the poorest of the poor to the leaders of countries, he had a remarkable way of connecting with young and old alike.

I have never been around anyone like him.

Romain gave us the general plan, and we added to it later. He told us we would be training about 30 coaches from around the country and would meet in Cotonou, the largest city in Benin, with a population of over two million.

The Benin Marina Hotel, the best hotel in the country, was one of the only places where you would see a white person and was visited by numerous foreign dignitaries and business people. It resembled a Hawaiian resort, located right on the ocean with a huge area that included a large pool and a dining area.

Romain said that we would have a full day to recover from our travel, then meet with the President and start our clinics for coaches.

What I knew of President Kerekou, who appeared to be in his 70s, was that he had been a dictator for over 30 years, like his close friend, Libyan revolutionary Muammar Gaddafi.

It was only after President Kerekou became a believer in Jesus that he allowed the government to become a democracy with a constitution similar to that of the United States. He lost the first election, but after five years, he was elected as the new president.

Romain told us the story of how he had first met President Kerekou. He had a vision he received from the Lord to share Jesus with him. Romain had never met Kerekou before, but during a heavily guarded event, he walked through security and right up to him.

It was an Apostle Paul-type event where God opened up the prison doors. Romain told the President that God had told him to share Jesus with him. From then on, they began meeting weekly and studying the Bible.

CHAPTER 3

A quiet and yet powerful presence

EACH OF THE SIX TIMES I brought our small groups to Benin, we would meet with the President upon our arrival and also the day of our flight home.

Prior to each meeting, we were escorted to a large hall and interviewed by the national TV station before and after our meeting.

Our meetings were always formal, and we were dressed in coats and ties. As with any meetings with heads of state, there are certain protocols. He sat in his regal chair while we, his guests, sat to his right and Romain sat on his left to interpret his words for us.

Depending on who was there, each spot was occupied the way President Kerekou wanted them to be seated. The first time I met with him was with my son Jeff and Al. When he walked in from an alcove, we all stood and were formally introduced. With a handshake, he greeted us individually and very warmly.

He was impeccably dressed in a dark suit and a buttoned-up Nehru-collar shirt. He wore shaded glasses and appeared very humble with a quiet and yet powerful presence, not what I expected from someone with his history. He spoke softly as Romain translated for him.

After a nice conversation in which President Kerekou expressed his appreciation for us being there, he said, "After you train our coaches, I want you to see and experience our country."

Once our meeting concluded, he asked for a very specific prayer — that whenever anyone came to visit, they would not bring demons with them. He asked us to pray that same prayer every time we met.

We were scheduled to do two basketball training sessions a day for nine days. Four times a day, we were driven 20 minutes from our hotel to an Olympic sports complex.

Our driver, François Tchokpodo, was a gracious, humble believer in Jesus. He was able to negotiate what we perceived as chaos with thousands of motor scooters, cars and trucks and nobody paying attention to traffic signals.

Years earlier, the Chinese had built an Olympic-scale complex for Benin in exchange for territorial fishing rights. It had a well-maintained soccer and track stadium, but the rest of the compound was rundown, with an Olympic-sized pool that looked like it had never been used.

The complex had a basketball arena that was used only for community events. With some renovation, I thought to myself, it could become one of the top athletic facilities in all of Africa.

Next to the basketball arena were two outdoor, black-topped basketball courts. The moveable steel-framed baskets had wooden backboards, but no nets, so we bought some.

Before the clinic began, we met with the coaches we were to train, 32 of them from all over the country. Most were in their 20s, and Romain told us that all but two of them were Muslim. He had asked us not to mention anything about Jesus until our final meeting on the 10th day.

The coach who organized the program, Aziz Adoumbou, was regarded as the best basketball player in the country. He had competed internationally and had founded a non-governmental national basketball program, known as an NGO.

There were four or five women who participated, one being Aziz's sister, who was a nurse and a good basketball player. A natural-born leader with tremendous enthusiasm, she easily competed against the guys.

Aziz also had two brothers at the clinic, both of whom were good players. Though he was somewhat weak in English, Aziz was my translator.

We taught the coaches the fundamentals and techniques of effective movement, shooting, dribbling and passing. We also taught the foundations for offense and defense through one-on-one, two-on-two, and three-on-three drills and competitions.

This led to five-on-five games, all of which my son Jeff participated in.

On the 10th day we met with all the coaches to wrap up our time together. Romain had said it was now time to reveal to the coaches why we had come to Benin. We sat in a small area of the stadium.

Romain told Al to lead off with an introduction, and told me to explain why we were there, and give my testimony. Romain said Jeff was to conclude our comments because everyone loved my son and really connected with him.

The night before we were to speak, Jeff was nervous and unsure of what he was going to say. I told him, "Just let the Lord express through you how you feel about being there."

Then we prayed together.

CHAPTER 4

The God you can talk to like a father

AFTER ROMAIN GAVE HIS OPENING REMARKS in French, all of the coaches stood up and shouted, "No, no, no!"

At the time, Jeff, Al and I didn't understand what Romain had said. Later, when we asked Romain, he laughed and said, "I told the coaches that I wanted to apologize to them, that I had made a mistake in bringing these coaches here. I said it looks like they have not done a good job and have not treated you well."

That's when they all jumped up and said, "No, no, no, that is not true!" When he asked them if they wanted to know why we were there, they all shouted in unison, "Oui!"

After Al's comments, I shared my faith in Jesus with them. I then told them about my first year of coaching at PLNU, and how difficult it was. I shared how I had prayed with my family before going into open-heart surgery, and that as I was being wheeled into the operating room, I prayed, "God, I'm in a win-win situation."

I told them that as I was going into surgery, I was praising and worshiping God for what He had done in my life. If I did not come out of the surgery, I would be in His presence, praising and worshiping Him. If I did come out of it, I would also be praising and worshiping Him.

Aziz's sister came up to me after I spoke and said, "I want to know the God you can talk to like a father."

A short time later, in the hotel dining room, we met with Romain and Aziz, along with his two brothers and sister. Romain had been asked by Aziz if he could tell them more about Jesus.

Romain opened up both the Koran and the Bible and then went through everything the Koran says about Jesus and contrasted that with what the Bible says about Him.

He built the case for Christ, and all four of them later would express faith in Jesus as Lord.

With the clinics completed, we would now travel through Benin, as the president wanted. We were provided a tour guide, who was a good friend of Romain, for our trip to the town of Ouidah, about an hour's drive from our hotel.

François drove us along the coast where we saw local kids surfing, like we would see in San Diego.

CHAPTER 5

The worst village in all of Benin

WE ARRIVED IN OUIDAH, which is located on the spot where the West African slave trade and voodoo originated. Our first stop was at the Portuguese fort that had been converted into a museum.

There, we learned that the region of Dahomey had been ruled by a king who captured his tribal enemies, and sacrificed them to his voodoo gods by throwing them off cliffs and using many other cruel methods.

When a Portuguese ship arrived in that area, the captain saw the king killing his enemies, and made a deal to buy them in exchange for trinkets. The Portuguese became the middlemen between the supplier — known as the voodoo kings — and the buyers.

The Portuguese built this fort where the slaves had been held before being transported to their ships. Before being shipped, they were chained up in buildings in total darkness so they would not know if it was day or night.

Rebellious slaves were punished severely by various methods of torture. If a slave got sick, they were buried alive.

In modern times, excavations of mass graves in Ouidah revealed thousands of human skeletons. The place was covered back up and made into a memorial.

At night, the chained slaves were force-marched from the fort to the ship. On the way to the ship the king had three voodoo curses placed on them. The first of the curses was placed when they were forced to walk around "The Tree of Forgetfulness" — nine times for men, seven times for women.

The curse was that they would not remember where they came from. The second was placed on them when they were forced to walk around another tree so they would have no desire to return.

From there, they went through what was called "the Gate of No Return." That curse was put on them so they could never return to their homeland.

A huge arch representing the gate stands there as a memorial. We felt the oppression and spiritual darkness. We prayed a lot.

The next day, Al, Jeff, Aziz, Romain, along with myself and a few others were driven by François to Akpali ("The Village of Jesus"), a village about an hour and a half north of Cotonou. We drove down a long dirt road and took a track into the bush.

Romain told us that he and the President agreed that this village had probably been the worst village in all of Benin. Romain had sent four young men that he was discipling into the village, which at that time was called "The Village of the Devil."

Filth was everywhere. The four young men went to serve the villagers by cleaning, organizing and working in the fields with the men of the village. Romain told the young men not to mention why they were there, the same thing he had told us before we started our clinics.

The young men served this village for a full year, walking two or three miles down a dirt track to get there each day.

When we arrived at Akpali, we were greeted by the entire village, decked out in their finest African-style attire. We met at a central meeting place where the villagers sat beneath a large, thatched canopy.

With Romain translating, the chief greeted us and told us the story of these four young men coming to the village. After a year, the chief told them, "You have shown that you love us. Now tell us why you are here."

They replied that they wanted to tell them about a person named Jesus of Nazareth. They shared the gospel in the language of the villagers while continuing their work.

As the chief recounted the story, one day the villagers were walking out to bury a girl of about 4 years of age when the four men met them on their way to the village. They were told that the girl had died, and that they were going to bury her.

The men then said, "God is the God of the living. We are going to pray for this girl to come back to life." They laid hands on her and prayed and, miraculously, she came back to life. The chief then said to us, "That girl is here and she wants to greet you."

At that moment, a young girl walked from her mother and shyly greeted us. Everyone in the village broke into singing and praising God.

We could see that the village had been transformed by the wonder of a girl being raised from the dead. The transformation included the chief and the witchdoctor. They gave up all their voodoo and ancestry worship and believed in Jesus.

When we looked around, the dirt grounds of the village of Akpali were raked clean. There were men's and women's separate toilet areas set up to provide privacy.

Where people had been dying from polluted water, they now had a new well dug for them by members of a church based in Texas. They had clean water and did not have to walk long distances to get it.

The transformation, joy and spirit of these people was overwhelming.

It was like we were walking with Jesus.

CHAPTER 6

We sensed an evil presence

WE LEFT AKPALI AND DROVE FURTHER up into the interior to the Palace of Abomey, where the Voodoo Kings of Dahomey reigned from the 16th century to the 19th century.

The palace was still much the same as when it was built. There were thick 15-foot-high walls around the compound. The walls had been built with the blood of the king's enemies. Instead of using water to make the bricks, they were made with blood.

When we walked into the compound, there was a huge thatched roof only a few feet off the ground. This is where the king was buried with his 20-some wives that he commanded to be killed for his burial. We were walking around and went into the pavilion where the king's throne was resting on four human skulls of chiefs he had killed.

Everything in that place was about voodoo and death.

The myth was that the king could change into a black jaguar, and that the jaguar then mated with the princess and that was how Africans came into existence. In the palace you see images of the jaguar, along with various voodoo and ritualistic artifacts.

Again, we sensed an evil presence that had once dominated much of Benin.

As the president wanted us to experience, I was seeing the history of his nation and the contrast between the dark powers of voodoo and the light of Jesus.

We kept traveling north and conducted basketball clinics, stopping at Four Square churches to meet with the elders and visit the president's hometown. That was our first trip. It only lasted 21 days, but I was forever changed.

Despite its darkness, I fell in love with Benin and its people. It felt like home to me, and after I left, I longed to return.

My son and I flew to Washington D.C. to give a report to Senator Inhofe and his chief of staff. As I was telling them what we had experienced, Sen. Inhofe said, "That's great, John, but I really want to hear from your son."

Jeff shared his thoughts and his experiences with him. A week after we got back to San Diego, Jeff got a call from Senator Inhofe's office saying that the senator wanted Jeff to return and work with him as an intern writer.

After short time, Jeff and I drove to D.C., with nearly all of his personal belongings.

While at PLNU, Jeff had connected with a gal, Leanna, who was a journalism major at PNLU, just as he had been. He was praying a lot about their relationship, and after a year, he left his position in D.C., returning to San Diego to court her. They would eventually marry.

PART 25

The Lord's Gym

CHAPTER 1

Hookers, drugs and gangs

SOON AFTER RETURNING FROM BENIN, I called my friend and former PLNU basketball player, Archie Ray Robinson, who was involved in the Young Life inner-city ministry.

I told him that I wanted to get involved, and he suggested that I contact his father, Pastor Archie Robinson. Archie invited me to attend "Pastor's Prayer," a group of pastors from Southeast San Diego. They met for prayer at Archie's church on Wednesday mornings.

I sat next to Pastor John Jacquess, who was also there for the first time. That was the beginning of a very special relationship between us.

In 2001, while I was still coaching at PLNU, my friends Milt and Karen Richards connected with The Lost Boys of Sudan, who were among thousands of homeless young boys whose parents had been murdered.

They traveled in the bush for years, living off the land, surviving the crossing of rivers, and wild animal attacks. Many of them had ended up in Kenyan refugee camps and Catholic Charities arranged to have them relocated to various cities around the U.S.

A small group came into San Diego where Karen Richards, who has always had a connection with Africans, reached out and got to know them. Early on, there were about five or six Lost Boys that Milt, Karen and I discipled.

Four of them moved into a house in Linda Vista with Dan Lickel, an attorney from our Thursday morning fellowship group.

Our four Lost Boys had a great desire to learn how to live in our American culture, and to learn more about God through the study of scriptures. They knew virtually nothing about living in this culture.

For instance, they would go to the freezer and throw frozen food away because they couldn't bite into it. They didn't know what it was because they had never used modern conveniences of any kind.

On Friday nights, Milt, Karen and I would go to the house where I would lead a Bible study, and Milt would teach practical living skills. They were eager to learn, but deeply wounded.

Over the course of time, those four went on to graduate from PLNU and have since become high achievers.

One evening, there was a gathering at the Lost Boy's house. My friend, Mark Yeeles, brought his guest, Billy Moore, who told me about the boxing charity he was running called ABC (Any Body Can), which was started by his father, legendary boxer Archie Moore.

Billy told me his gym was located nearby in a small storefront on Imperial Boulevard, so I went there and checked out the program.

While we were watching his boxers train in a dilapidated boxing ring, Billy told me that World Gym on Market Street had recently gone into bankruptcy. He said they had a nearly new boxing ring there and asked me to go with him to meet the owner of the property to see if he would donate or sell it to ABC.

The gym was a 33,000 square foot facility with equipment that seemed barely used. We met with the owner, Dan Furlan, and as we left to enter the gym to check out the boxing ring, I saw rows of cardio equipment, administrative offices, and an aerobic classroom.

Something came over me and I said to Dan, "Let's talk about leasing the entire gym." He gave a hesitant okay.

As soon as I left there, I called my friend, Tyler Miller, who had been involved in Oakbridge and its funding. He had recently told me, "If you ever get involved in anything else, let me know."

When I talked with Tyler about starting an inner-city ministry in the gym, that led to a second meeting with Tyler, Dan, Billy and myself.

We agreed that we would pay monthly rent on a graduated basis over the next couple of years. That led to the founding of the non-profit Lord's Fitness and Community Development Center. Dan Furlan, the building's owner, really liked our idea.

The area where the gym was located, at the corner of Market and 43rd Street, was filled with hookers, drugs and gangs. To the north were the Crips, to the south were the Bloods, to the east was the Lincoln Gang. And to the west, there was a huge cemetery where many of the kids killed in gang violence were buried.

It was a very dark area.

CHAPTER 2

Everybody knows this is a safe place

PASTOR JACQUESS LIVED TWO BLOCKS AWAY, and said he had been praying that the building would become a church. He said the area was so bad that they wouldn't let their kids walk the four blocks to school or even go into their own front yards.

One late night when we were fixing up the gym before the opening, we heard shots fired across the street. I thought, whoa, this is a tough area.

Monroe Nash, a San Diego basketball legend, had played basketball at USC after me. He had visited me at PLNU a year earlier, and let me know he wanted to be involved with me in whatever I did in the future.

Monroe became the business administrator of Lord's Fitness Center (LFC), and Archie Ray became the gym's manager.

The rent had been $22,000 a month, and we negotiated a contract to pay $8,000 a month for the first six months, increasing to $10,000 a month the next six months, and $22,000 a month from there on.

We were going to run it as a fitness center with the idea that memberships would help pay the rent. My hope was to get the many churches in the area to unify and be a part of the LFC ministry.

It didn't happen.

After a year, it was becoming evident that we couldn't make or raise enough money to pay our rent. Dan Furlan and I had developed a great relationship, yet a couple of years later, I had to tell him we couldn't pay the full rent.

When we met at his home, he told me, "Don't worry about the rent."

For the next four years, he forgave the entire $22,000 a month rent. He said he really appreciated what we were doing, and that the whole community had changed for the better because of our presence.

As soon as LFC was up and running, we moved Pastor's Prayer to what we called "the upper room." The light of the Lord at LFC, the prayers of the pastors, and us walking the area pushed the darkness out.

Here was a 33,000-square-foot building in the heart of gang territory, and in those five years it was never tagged by graffiti.

One day, we moved a lot of exercise equipment to put in a stage and chairs for a public worship time. Pastor Archie Robinson and other church musicians led the worship. There were over 50 people worshiping God while some others were working out in other parts of the gym.

During the singing, a young man came running in sweating and panicked and asked Pastor Jacquess what was going on. He replied by asking what was going on with him.

The young man replied, "I was running for my life from gang members and came in here because everybody knows this is a safe place." Pastor Jacquess presented the gospel to him and the young man came to know the Lord Jesus right then and there.

Afterward, Pastor Jacquess said to me, "This gym is worth that one soul being saved."

There was a former college professor I got to know who held classes not far from the gym. He had a passion for teaching and mentoring struggling high school students and had started an independent study program.

He told me a story about a tall sophomore basketball player from Lincoln High who wanted to go to college and play in the NBA. He was struggling academically when the professor asked him to prepare a presentation to the class on how to shoot a basketball. The professor had given the player's classmates questions to ask him when he was finished with his presentation.

The questions were related to what the difference was between shooting layups, free throws and three-point shots.

When the class was over, the player asked how he did. The professor said, "I gave you a B on presentation and an A on physics." "An A in physics?" the player responded. The professor explained to him that he had taught about arc and thrust and levers.

The light went on, and the basketball player went on to become an excellent student who attended college on an academic scholarship while also playing D-1 basketball.

That story motivated me to continue developing our educational and mentoring programs.

The Lord's Fitness Center became a big part of my life and I was there almost every day. I would even ride my bicycle there from our home in Point Loma — a 20-mile round trip.

After we had been in operation for about a year, Billy Moore, who had been running his ABC program out of our boxing facility at LFC, set up a meeting with his pastor and me.

The pastor said, "I believe Billy should be making as much money as you." I leaned forward in my chair and said, "I agree 100 percent. He should be making as much as me."

Then he asked me, "How much are you making?"

I said, "I don't take a dime out of this gym and I'm not on salary. This whole thing is God's work, and I'm doing it for Him."

Both Billy and the pastor were speechless.

CHAPTER 3

A bucket of water, some soap and a towel

MILT RICHARDS HAD A FRIEND, Charles Mendies, who was overseeing a ministry in Nepal and had been thrown in prison for his faith.

Mother Theresa had asked Charles to travel with her toward the end of her life. When Charles came to San Diego, Milt and I and a few others met him for dinner at Ki's Restaurant in Encinitas, one of our favorite gathering spots.

One of the most impactful things he told us was that our expectations of others often get in the way of what the Lord is wanting to do. I had been dealing with my own expectations that I had put on Billy Moore, and the Lord just pierced me with that thought.

I called Billy that night and asked him to meet me the next morning before the gym opened. Before he got there, I got a bucket of water, some soap and a towel. I asked him to sit down and told him that I had hindered him because of my expectations.

I asked for his forgiveness and told him that the Lord had impressed upon me to wash his feet.

He said, "There's no way you're going to do that," and I replied, "If the Lord wants me to do something, I'm going to do it."

When he hesitantly agreed, I said, "This is in the name of Jesus," and I washed his feet. He said he understood and our relationship improved.

Every Tuesday morning, LFC leadership, Milt and I met for fellowship and prayer in the upper room. One day, Archie Ray Robinson brought up a concern he had for Morse High, a school a few miles from us.

He said there was something mysterious going on there that no one could figure out, almost like a curse. I immediately said, "Let's go over there and pray."

I called Pastor Robinson and Pastor Jacquess, and told them about our conversation and asked them to meet us at LFC and go to Morse. They dropped everything and we drove to Morse.

At the principal's office, we told him, "We're pastors and friends in the neighborhood and would like to walk your campus and pray. Is that okay?" He gave us his consent and guest passes.

When we started walking around, the feeling of oppression was like being back in Ouidah. We prayed and came against the powers of darkness. It was a dark, cloudy day, but when we had almost finished walking the campus, blue skies opened up and the sun came out, shining on us.

It was like receiving God's blessing for our obedience.

CHAPTER 4

Our careers were parallel

AFTER FIVE YEARS OF HELPING US and seeing the community change for the better, Dan Furlan told me, "John, it's been fantastic having you here, but I'm selling all my properties, including the Lord's Fitness Center building, and moving to the Dominican Republic."

There was no way we could afford to buy the building. We looked around for other places, but we had to make the decision to close LFC down. We had lasted from 2003 to 2008, and we had built a full-sized basketball court in the parking lot and organized weekend league games.

We gave opportunity to groups like Steps of Praise, a faith-based dance group led by Pastor Adrian Ewings. They began using the aerobic room at the gym to practice their dance routines, and hold events at LFC.

The Robinson brothers, all of whom worked at LFC, had formed a band called "Those Dang Robinsons." Along with various other musical artists, they gave many great concerts on the property. Mobile health units came by to give free screenings.

Many young athletic trainers got their start at Lord's Fitness. We had a day-care program and gave out snacks after school. The many relationships formed through LFC have yielded much fruit.

The experiences and the friends I made there continue to impact my life by deepening my faith and relationship with Jesus. I still continue to meet weekly for Pastor's Prayer via Zoom.

During my entire time working at LFC, I was traveling to Benin each summer. After my first trip to Benin, it was important to me to bring an African-American there to get their perspective and see how they would respond to the experience.

I connected with Steve Johnson, a 6-10 African American who had played in the NBA. Though his career came after mine, our careers were parallel in some ways. He played in the league for 10 years on seven different teams and was an All-Star. Steve and his son, Marcus, agreed to come along on our next trip.

Through Milt Richards, I got to know Marty Sherman, who is very connected to The Fellowship. I had worked with his son on his basketball skills at his home in Annapolis, and Marty suggested that the Davidson family go with us to Benin.

Jim Davidson, his wife Bunnie, their daughter, Diana, and their son, Jimmy, became part of our team. Steve Abraham, who had traveled with me to Spain and was now a youth pastor, was also on the trip along with Steve Johnson, his son Marcus, my son Jeff, and Al Nordquist.

The plan was to do most everything we had done on the first trip, but this time we were able to use the Olympic complex's arena.

The only problem was that we had to bring the outdoor baskets inside. These were old, metal pipe basketball standards with wooden backboards that required many people to carry, but we managed to do it.

On the previous trip, we had trained coaches, but on this trip, we did day camps every day for a week for 40 to 50 kids. I was beginning to get a feel for the largely untapped basketball abilities of the young athletes throughout the country.

President Kerekou set up a meeting with a Benin cabinet member who oversaw the country's sports programs. Soccer ruled the sports world there, and we later found out that whatever money was allotted for basketball was siphoned off for soccer.

What was emerging through my deepening relationship with my coaching friend Aziz was the idea of putting together a non-profit organization for basketball similar to the AAU in the U.S. We also had the dream of forming a basketball and educational academy. That would continue taking shape over my next trips to Benin.

The idea became a dream that continued for some time.

As with many short-term mission trips, many of those who go are often more deeply affected than those they came to serve. Once Steve Johnson saw where slavery and voodoo began and went to the places where curses were put on slaves, it changed the direction of his life.

CHAPTER 5

'We deal with demons every day'

RICK ARCHER, WHO CO-FOUNDED one of the largest architectural firms in Texas and runs his business on the teachings of Jesus, joined us on a later trip to Benin.

He was to assess a 100-hectare property that I'd envisioned as the future site of a West African sports academy near the president's hometown.

Reggie and Stacy Williams, who had both been adopted as children and traced their lineage to slaves, also came on the trip. I had been praying about someone to come alongside me who understood the vision and spoke French, and Reggie looked like that someone. I had coached against him when he played at Westmont College, and later when he became a coach.

We also took Milt Richards and Harry Hosmer, the founder of a publicly-traded oil company called Royal Energy.

As on previous trips, the first thing we did was meet again with the President. We met to introduce my friends and talk about what we were going to do and where we were going to travel. As he always did, the President asked for prayer.

Sometime after that meeting, Romain set up a dinner in a private home for Harry, Milt and me to meet with leaders in various fields from the cities of Cotonou, Porto Novo, and Calavi.

There was the top TV personality, who told the most amazing story of God intervening in his life, followed by a few Army generals and two university presidents.

When the president of Calavi University asked us how we dealt with demonic influences in the U.S., Harry said to the group, "I've got this. We name it and then we prescribe drugs against it."

Hearing that, the university president said, "That's amazing. We deal with demons every day in our classrooms."

While we were at our dinner meeting, Reggie, Rick, and Stacy were being toured around the city by a man who was visiting from Ghana. He drove them by the president's personal home and said it would be okay to take photos.

Reggie began taking pictures of the president's home, and they were immediately confronted by army police who took them into custody, and detained them at the police station for hours.

The army was very protective of the president and they were protecting his home.

Romain got a call from Rick who told him they were being detained by the police. Romain talked to the chief of police, who was a relative of President Kerekou, to obtain their release.

A short time after, we started our trip and headed for our first stop, Akpali. We saw a small medical building with no medical supplies, along with a regional school, that had been built there.

These were brick structures with solid roofs, unlike the huts with thatched roofs and dirt floors which we saw on our first trip.

Since our last visit, it was clear that progress had been made.

CHAPTER 6

'She was as unto death'

IT WAS SUNDAY MORNING WHEN WE MET with all the villagers in a large classroom where church gatherings were being held.

We sat in front, facing the congregation, while Romain stood off to our right, translating. The village chief, whom I had met on my other trips, and the former witchdoctor were there.

The chief welcomed us and told a brief history of the village and the young men who had come to serve the people of the village.

He then introduced the school principal, who told us a story. He said, "Two weeks ago today, a mother accompanied by her young son carried her daughter, who was about 6 years old, into one of our classrooms."

The exact language of the teacher was "She was as unto death," but Romain translated and said she was dead. The principal, the mother and her younger son then laid hands on the girl and prayed that she would come back to life.

She started breathing, but she remained in a coma.

They drove her a long way on dirt roads to the hospital on a motor scooter. The principal continued his story, saying, "A few days ago when we found out you were coming, we said, 'We need to pray that she comes out of her coma so she can be here with you.' So, we prayed for her, she came out of her coma, and we brought her back home."

Then he said, "I would like to have her come up here and greet you in the name of Jesus."

When she came up and greeted us, the spirit of God was so present that we all felt it.

Stacy Williams, who was seated next to me, began to cry. She said, "May I say something?" She rose, went to the girl, went to her knees, put her arm around her and said, "Two weeks ago today, I was in church in Santa Barbara, California. We were worshiping God when I had a vision of a girl and the Lord said, 'Pray for this girl.'"

Stacy began praying for her family and her situation, and the Lord said, "No, pray that she might live." Then Stacy told us, "This is the girl in my vision! The Lord wants you to know that He sees you and that you are known, even in California."

The entire congregation started weeping with joy. Romain turned to me and said, "Now what?" I said, "Well, I think we should worship God." They picked up their homemade drums and stringed instruments and we proceeded to worship.

CHAPTER 7

'Please forgive me'

WE HAD ALL EXPERIENCED SOMETHING we would never forget. We were in the presence of Jesus, getting a glimpse into heaven.

That same day, we travelled to a larger village that consisted of two different tribes. There was another young man whom Romain had sent into that village. He started doing what the four young men had done in Akpali.

Through that, he was able to share the gospel. When we got there, we were seated in a large open area surrounded by most of the people in the village.

The village chief told us a brief history of the village, which was that the two tribes hated each other. More than a hundred years earlier, ancestors of one tribe had sold members of the other tribe into slavery.

The young man came to the village to serve and teach the gospel of Jesus Christ, and over time God reconciled the tribes to each other.

Having just been moved by the Spirit of the Lord in Akpali, our group was experiencing that same move of God now.

At that moment, Rick Archer, who was raised in Texas, stood up and said, "I grew up in an area where my ancestors bought and had slaves. I want to ask forgiveness for myself and my ancestors."

Rick dropped to his knees on the dirt in front of them all and said, "Please forgive me." There was a mother sitting near me with two children. I saw her talk to them, and they got up, walked over to Rick and hugged him.

It was a picture burned forever in my heart. Tears flowed throughout the congregation.

We were extremely emotional, and this was only the first day of our trip to the north.

From there, we traveled to other towns to conduct basketball clinics with coaches and players, including visits with pastors and leaders of Four Square Churches. We ended up in the President's hometown to see for ourselves the 100-hectare property that President Kerekou had suggested for the academy.

Reggie Williams, Rick and I walked the whole property. A river ran through the partially forested property with some villagers farming a section of it. It was perfect for the vision we had. We all agreed that it should be built with African-styled architecture, not Western.

As for Rick, he was in architectural heaven.

However, we learned that if you want to buy property in Benin, you have to first deal with the village chief. He can either give permission for use, where you never fully own the property, or you can purchase it outright and have full legal title.

CHAPTER 8

Dressed like Southern belles

ON ONE OF MY TRIPS TO BENIN, there was a group from Ghana that had also traveled to meet with President Kerekou.

Among them was Ghana's largest chicken farmer and Ronnie Cameron, one of the largest chicken farmers in the U.S. The translator for the meeting was Ron Weeks, who was part of The Fellowship. He had grown up in Congo and could translate in French and various African dialects.

Romain said that the President wanted me to attend, as well, and I sat next to Ron. The president was talking to Romain, who was translating for us when Ron leaned over and said, "Romain did not accurately translate what the President had said."

He said the president was speaking highly of Romain, but that Romain changed the wording, so that the words weren't as flattering. Romain is one of the most humble and gifted men I have ever met in my life.

As in every meeting I had with the President, which was at least twice on every trip, he again asked us to pray that demonic spirits would not enter the room.

President Kerekou and Romain wanted me to be with them in meeting with two black women who came from the South in the United States. They came into the meeting dressed like Southern belles. The president asked why they were there, and they told him.

In so many words, the president replied, "What do you mean by coming here and telling us what you are going to do for us, rather than asking us what we need? No, you are not going to do that here."

On another occasion, Romain asked me to attend a meeting at the Benin Marina Hotel. We were meeting with the advance man for an evangelist from the U.S., who wanted to do a crusade in Benin. I was there just to listen. This man presented a proposal for the evangelist's proposed crusade.

Benin would have to buy an unreasonable number of his books, pay the expenses of the evangelist, and make many other provisions for him. Romain listened closely and then said, in essence, "I'm sorry, you won't be coming into this country."

In Benin and surrounding countries, the main religions are animism, voodoo and ancestral worship. Romain explained that when evangelists hold their crusades and preach the gospel, many of the people at the crusades go forward to improve their chances of going to heaven.

They say they believe in Jesus, but are not discipled, and so they hang on to their animism, voodoo and ancestral practices. The scriptures are the only word of God, and that's not always taught to new believers in Jesus.

My experiences in Benin were like being in the first-century church. Those who had been discipled in the Word of God, the Bible, were taught about their new life in Jesus. They trusted in what the Word says, praying for provision, healing, and for people to come back to life.

There are many in America who could learn from those believers in Benin.

CHAPTER 9

Against Margie's advice

PRESIDENT KEREKOU TOLD ME THAT HE WANTED his 16-year-old daughter, Sephora, to be educated in the United States.

He then told that he'd like me to serve as her legal guardian until she was 18 and attending college, so she came to San Diego and lived with Margie and me for a few months. I was humbled by his request and that he would trust us with his daughter.

For starters, I helped her enroll in a top ESL program (English as a Second Language) at Cal State San Marcos. Then I arranged for her to live with a family while she was attending school, and helped mentor her in the ways of American culture. As her legal guardian, I had to be there when she set up a checking account and when she bought a cell phone.

She was highly intelligent and ended up being first in her class. I helped her decide what she would study in college and suggested that she study international economics. She went on to attend New York University before getting her master's at Yale. She continues to live in New York City.

Our fifth trip to Benin was basically for business and for attending President Kerekou's International Reconciliation Conference. A friend and businessman, Greg Schneider, planned on attending along with Al Nordquist.

On the day we were to leave, Al woke up with a health scare and he and his wife decided that he shouldn't go. For me, the thought of going without Al was like Moses without Aaron. He was my covenant brother, and we always had each other's backs.

Against Margie's advice, I still went.

Soon after our arrival in Benin, Greg and I were invited to a dinner meeting at the U.S. embassy that Romain and Ambassador Neill had set up with some of the country's most prominent business leaders.

About 15 of us met and I cast the vision for the academy and the national basketball program. That led us to visiting many of the businesses owned by these men.

Greg and I learned more about the complex economics of the country, and I was trying to ascertain if building an academy and national basketball program could be accomplished without the need for government funding.

We traveled throughout the area, looking at the basketball infrastructure and found there were only about 10 public courts in the cities of Cotonou, Puerto-Novo, and Calavi, home to a few million people among them.

I had a business plan, but soon realized that without my being in the country on a full-time basis, that plan didn't have a chance of coming to fruition.

We also attended the Benin Reconciliation and Development Convention, along with various leaders from African nations and the Western World. The weeklong convention was highlighted by an "Apology" ceremony.

In his moving message, President Kerekou apologized to the Western world for his country's role in the enslavement of their own people, which perpetuated the slave trade.

When I returned from this trip, I was extremely sick with a high fever. Before the Wednesday morning pastor's prayer meeting at LFC, I contacted Pastor Jacquess.

I told him that I was really sick and couldn't make prayer, but he told me to get out of bed and get down there immediately. When I walked through the door, into their prayer meeting, Pastor Jacquess said, "You've come back with some attachments."

They had me sit in the center of the room, and about 15 pastors laid hands on me and prayed for my release from whatever spirits were binding me. I was healed on the spot. Lesson learned.

I believe that without the covering of my covenant brother Al Nordquist by my side, I was made more vulnerable to demonic influence and oppression.

CHAPTER 10

There's no skiing in West Africa

GREG FRANCIS, AN AUSTRALIAN whom I met through Milt Richards, accompanied me on my last trip to Africa, along with Ron Weeks and Lynette Boggs, an African American who was then a Las Vegas councilwoman.

We first went to Accra, the capital of Ghana, where Ron had started various men's groups based on The Fellowship model. He was involved in starting the Youth Corps, a discipleship movement for impoverished youth. We met with some of those involved in Youth Corps along with business and political leaders.

Because of my newly-fused ankle and severe neuropathy, I took trekking poles to help me walk. Throughout the trip the local people noticed me and kiddingly said, "There's no skiing in West Africa."

From Accra we drove to Cotonou, Benin. Once there, we met with Romain and Luc Gnacadja, an architect who was running for president of Benin. There, we were told that the property where we planned to build the academy was no longer available.

We took Lynette to Ouidah to visit the Portuguese fort and other sites where the curses were put on the slaves. I'll never forget her walking through the Gate of No Return with Greg and me. We prayed for her ancestral curses to be broken.

She fell to her knees, weeping, knowing that the curses had been broken in her life and that of her family.

Toward the end of what proved to be my final trip to Benin, several events unfolded that altered the next chapters of my life.

President Kerekou's two terms were up, my friend Luc lost the presidential election, our proposed academy property fell through, and the U.S. Ambassador, who had encouraged our master plan, was being replaced.

Benin's newly elected president didn't want to have anything to do with what we had started. It seemed like the Benin chapter of my life had ended.

I wondered, what was God going to do with me? Plenty, as it turned out.

A scripture comes to mind from the book of Proverbs that says, *"In his heart a man plans his course, but the Lord determines his steps"* (Proverbs 16:9 NIV).

PART 26

Africa came to me

CHAPTER 1

The vision the Lord gave me

My entire life to this point has been built on building blocks.

My being pulled out of baseball and put into basketball led to a college career. That led me to meet Don Williams, which in turn led me to Harlem. If I had never gone to Harlem, I doubt I would have become the player I became.

The NBA became an economic tool and provided me with resources that helped build the Kingdom of God.

From the NBA, I was led to start Oakbridge and an Arabian horse ranch. From there, I was led to turn around various college basketball programs. That led to my spreading the Gospel through basketball to a number of different countries.

I was led to the inner-city of Southeast San Diego where we started and ran the Lord's Fitness and Development Center. At that same time, I was traveling to Benin with a vision to build a national basketball program for the country.

After Benin, through Pastor Tim Timmons and Milt Richards, I met a young man named TJ Doyle. He had started a basketball management agency ɔr college players who had the desire to play professionally. TJ asked me to ɛlp disciple him as he navigated the world of professional sports.

In 2009, I spent four days a week for six weeks training his players before the NBA Draft in Las Vegas. I also traveled with TJ to evaluate different players.

I shared my vision of the academy in Benin with him, which led to the idea of an academy to train players for the NBA. We attempted to start a basketball academy in San Diego and also bring an NBA D-league team here, neither of which panned out.

After that, TJ and some of his investor friends bought a top-rated professional Spanish team in Seville that had an academy associated with it. The idea was to bring in African players to prepare them through the academy to play in the Spanish league with hopes that they would go on to play in the NBA.

Then Milt and I talked about starting an academy in connection with a pro basketball team in his hometown of Adelaide, Australia. We spent a year taking trips to Australia and it looked like our plans were coming together, but they, too, fell apart.

It appeared that the vision the Lord gave me for a basketball academy would not be accomplished.

Just a few months later, Milt had a stroke and died, perhaps as a result of our failed Australian venture. My friend had deep and lasting impact on my life and countless others around the world.

That spring, I got a call from one of my former players, Willie Brisco. He told me a very difficult story of a high school basketball player, Kofi Cofi, from Ghana. Willie asked me to try and help Kofi and his sponsor family, Eric and Shannon Vajda, figure out his situation.

It didn't work out for a number of reasons, and he ended up going back to Ghana.

At his going-away party, at the Vajda home, I met the coach responsible for bringing Kofi over, Kwaku Amoaku. I sat with Mike Howell with his son,

Chris, who was then a 14-year-old freshman at San Marcos High, and a point guard on the basketball team.

I asked him what his strengths and weaknesses were. His dad answered that his son's strengths were that he was smart and could handle the ball. He said his weaknesses were making free throws, and finishing inside.

I immediately knew what his problem was and asked if he wanted to learn to shoot, right then. The Vajdas had a backyard basketball court, but it was dark outside.

We went to the court and Mike used the light from his cell phone while I showed Chris what his problem was in his shooting technique. He was a great learner and improved on the spot, which led to my coaching and mentoring him.

I became very involved with Chris and his family and continue teaching and mentoring him to this day.

At this writing, he is a redshirt freshman with a great coach, Randy Bennett, at St. Mary's College in Northern California.

Through the Vajdas and Kwaku, I began working with other African players. I wasn't going around the world, trying to work with African players. Instead, African players were coming to me.

Through contacts in Ghana, I was asked by a basketball coach who was also a youth pastor to help him coach a 6-11 African player. Using an iPhone and Facetime we were able to connect on the court. I would make a comment and the coach in Ghana would relate it to his player.

It was unique and it worked, and continues to work today.

CHAPTER 2

One of the most memorable things

IN THE EARLY 2000s, while I was recovering from one of my many back injuries, San Diego area Young Life director Eric Scofield, and Mike Curran, Young Life's beach cities director, invited me to join the San Diego area board.

They wanted me to help disciple some of Young Life's adult directors.

One of those directors, Luke Walther, had just moved to town after attending Wheaton College and graduating from Westmont College. I was led to study Jesus' Sermon on the Mount in the Book of Mathew. After meeting every Tuesday for at least three hours, we finished the study in seven months.

We agreed that it was one of the most memorable things either of us had ever experienced.

I remembered what I said to Don Williams when he was teaching me how to pray and study the Bible, "I hope that one day I'll do what you're doing."

I have continued my relationship with Ron Weeks, whom I had met through President Kerekou in Benin. Ron, who grew up in a missionary family in Mbandaka, Congo, traveled with me to Ghana.

Inspired by Ron and his wife, Doris, and their commitment to God's call, I was moved to revive the Lord's Fitness Center's nonprofit corporation to support Ron and Doris' mission to Congo. Al Arias, who had helped set up LFC, also helped with reforming and naming this new ministry.

Together, we changed the name to Redemption Works International (RWI).

Doris started an English training school and Bible school in Mbandaka, while Ron teaches "Farming God's Way," a Biblical way to produce better crops, throughout the region.

He sometimes travels 125 miles on the Congo River in a large motorized canoe, and using a solar panel and a battery, he also presents "The Jesus Film" to villagers.

Now he has a new device that provides an audio version of the New Testament, spoken in their native language, that he gives to leaders of the villages.

For me, it's rewarding and inspiring that he continues to impact the lives of the villagers.

CHAPTER 3

Amazingly intricate detail

ONE AFTERNOON IN EARLY 2020, I got a call from Yauhen Massalski, a 6-10 center from Belarus who was playing for USD.

He was entering his senior year when he called former USD head coach Brad Holland to say that after three years as a starter, he believed he hadn't learned how to be a better basketball player.

He asked for Coach Holland's advice and was told to call me immediately, which he did. Yauhen, who went by the nickname "Squirrel," explained his situation and asked if I would help him.

I told him I'd be happy to do so.

Through the use of an online subscription program called Synergy, which breaks down every D-1 college game into amazingly intricate detail, we began to analyze his game together. As a player, he had access to the program, which allowed us to watch every facet of his game together via Zoom.

I quickly saw that his assessment of his play was accurate. Year by year, he clearly had digressed.

I had him place his iPhone on a tripod so we could see each other, and through earphones he was able to hear me. I trained and taught him this way for over a year and a half, plus twice in person.

I had to rebuild his entire game. First, I taught him how to build his athleticism in every way by jumping rope.

Then, I taught him how to shoot with perfect technique, how to finish shots near the basket, how to block shots, pass, and offensively and defensively rebound, and how to play half-court basketball with maximum effectiveness and precision.

He took notes on everything I taught him, and he's one of the hardest workers I've ever coached, which has been very gratifying.

When his senior year at USD began, we watched videos of his practices and games. It was a bad Covid year for the team, and Squirrel didn't get to play much until the last game of the season, in which he scored 33 points.

After seeking my counsel, Squirrel decided to play his fifth year of eligibility at the University of San Francisco (USF). It was a great move, and we continued evaluating his play on Synergy during the season.

The end result was that USF put together its best record in years, and he was named first-team, all-conference. A lot of NBA teams were interested in him and USF was going to the NCAA playoffs, but he blew his knee out during the last game of the regular season.

Since then, he's undergone three surgeries, but he's determined to make a comeback as a pro player, either in the U.S. or overseas.

Squirrel and I continue to communicate, with him asking me for advice and encouragement, which I'm always happy to provide.

Around that time, I met virtually with Akol Lem, a 17-year-old Sudanese player who lives in Nairobi, Kenya, through Terry Bennett, whom I had coached at Bethany. I am now coaching and teaching Akol online, as I did with Yauhen, each of us adjusting to the ten-hour time difference between San Diego and Kenya.

In addition, through my relationship with Doug Burleigh, I've been mentoring and discipling coaches in Russia and Kazakhstan, all from my home via Zoom.

CHAPTER 4

You don't want to tell me I can't do something

I'VE ALWAYS BELIEVED THAT if you seek to be the best, then seek the best to teach you.

I've done that in sports and in life. When I decided coaching basketball was going to be my career, I contacted the best coaches and mentors in the country, John Wooden and Pete Newell.

A couple of years before I was married, I was playing golf with Bill Westphal and Jim Ferguson, a high school youth pastor from Hollywood Presbyterian church. Bill and Jim would beat me every time we played.

One day, Jim said, "If you beat me once in the next ten times, I'll take you and Margie to dinner anywhere you like." I took that as a major challenge and got in touch with former PGA pro Jerry Barber's son, Tom, the golf pro at Griffith Park.

Jerry was the oldest man to ever win the Open in Great Britain, and his son was a tremendous teacher. I only took two lessons from Tom, and he said, "I am only going to teach you two things — stance and how to grip the club. Don't let anyone ever try to change your swing."

That tip alone took ten strokes off my game, and I began shooting in the 80s. When I played Jim again, I was up a couple of strokes going into the last hole of our second match.

Before I stepped up to hit my drive, Jim said, "Wait a minute." He then took a ten-dollar bill out of his pocket, and stuck the tee with the ball on it, piercing the bill.

As I was addressing my ball, Jim said, "If you outdrive me on this hole, this ten-dollar bill is yours."

That was some gamesmanship.

After I outdrove him by 50 yards, I pocketed the ten bucks and beat h. for the first time. You don't want to tell me I can't do something.

After I retired from the NBA, I played a lot of tennis matches against my former teammate Toby Kimball, who had retired two years before I did.

At 6-8, Toby was an excellent tennis player and won every match we played against each other.

I thought, this has got to stop.

Right away, I got in touch with Dennis Ralston, who was a tremendous pro tennis player from USC and later became the teaching pro coach at Mission Hills Country Club in Rancho Mirage. I asked him whom he thought was the best tennis coach in San Diego.

Dennis introduced me to the pro at Lomas Santa Fe Country Club, and for four months I took lessons every week. Between lessons, I did nothing but practice. I didn't play a match for months, not until the next time against Toby.

That time, I beat him, and our on-court battles went on for several more years.

Another time, when Dennis was coaching my friend, Stan Smith, at Mission Hills CC, he invited Margie and me to join them. He said to be sure to bring my racket.

When we arrived, Dennis said, "Okay, I'm gonna find out how good you really are."

He set up a match with me against the club's reigning champion, and the next day we played on a court next to where Dennis and Stan were training.

I got drilled in the first set, 6-1.

Seeing that, Dennis, who knew I had a strong serve, called me over. He said, "I thought you were a smart guy. Don't you realize that he loves speed? Start using your junk serve."

I did, and won the next set, but I lost in a tie-breaker in the third, to lose the match.

But I was exhilarated to be competitive at that high level of play.

Another time, I teamed up with Stan as part of his Stan Smith Tennis Camp that we held at Oakbridge. We played against the Mayer brothers, Sandy and Gene, then ranked as the world's top doubles team.

I knew I couldn't come close to their world-class talent, but it was sure fun being competitive with them.

After my NBA career was over, I took up racquetball, which was then growing in popularity. I decided to learn from the game's best player, Bud Muelheisen, who had been the San Diego Rockets' team dentist.

Dr. Bud, who is credited with inventing racquetball in the early 1970s, taught me proper technique, strategy, and how to practice.

As I did with tennis, I practiced and practiced until I became a competitive racquetball player.

In fact, I once played in a pro-am celebrity tournament, where I reached the money round by beating Hall of Fame third baseman Brooks Robinson. One of the great thrills of my life was playing against Brooks and having lunch with him afterwards.

So, I guess you could say that I was a pro racquetball player, too.

Same thing with volleyball, sort of. In 1980, I signed a contract to play for a San Diego-based pro volleyball team, but the team folded before that season began.

CHAPTER 5

"I'm a competitive athlete again"

BACK IN THE SUMMER MONTHS OF 2020, my shoulder was causing me so much discomfort and pain that I was no longer able to hit a golf ball or throw a ball.

I could hardly move my shoulder at all. It hurt so much that I wasn't even able to ride my bike.

It was becoming very discouraging. I couldn't do much of anything physically, except maybe walk, but not for too long or very far.

Feeling desperate, I went to an orthopedic surgeon at Scripps Clinic in La Jolla, who told me that it was time for me to get a full shoulder replacement. That would be in addition to my new left ankle and new right hip, among my 31 lifetime surgeries.

Because I'd had so many previous surgeries, I'd been putting this one off for years.

Now, I was told there was no more time to waste.

I was scheduled for surgery in early December 2021, but in October I was in so much back pain that I was bed-ridden. I couldn't get out of bed without excruciating pain, the worst pain I've ever suffered.

This was getting really serious, and I asked Margie to call an ambulance to take me to the hospital. There, I was diagnosed with a severe infection of the bones in my lower back.

No one could figure out how that had happened, but they started giving me a heavy intravenous dose of antibiotics. I spent the next four and a half days in the hospital, flat on my back.

When I came home, I still had an intravenous line in my arm. I had to use walker to get around, and my whole body was very weak. Margie had to give me a huge dose of antibiotics every day for the next five weeks. Meanwhile, my shoulder surgery was postponed to April 2021.

Despite all that, I knew that I'd always been a fierce warrior, a competitive battler. There's no "give up" in me. I was *not* going to let my condition stop me from making a full recovery.

But it was really hard.

After three months or so, I recovered enough to get slightly more movement in my shoulder.

In June, two Point Loma friends of mine — John Freeman, who served as this book's editor, and Dr. Ned Chambers — invited me to come to the San Diego Yacht Club to watch them play a game called pickleball, which I knew nothing about.

Curious, I got in touch with my surgeon and asked him what he thought about me trying to play the game. He said I'd be fine, but to avoid hitting overheads.

When I asked Dr. Ned if he could recommend a teaching pro to help me get started, he suggested that I contact Jay Parker, a respected local pro and Navy veteran, which I did. After three lessons, I was totally hooked on pickleball.

Even with my limited mobility, I was convinced that I could play and, most exciting of all, compete. Then, as I'd done before, many, many times, I practiced and practiced before I played my first match. I watched countless videos on strategy and technique, over and over.

I started playing on a semi-regular basis at the San Diego Tennis & Racquet Club and discovered that I had some innate skills because I'd played plenty of tennis, ping pong and racquetball over the years.

I was really excited.

One of the players at the club who was my age was an outstanding, nationally-ranked pickleball player, Fred Shuey. By coincidence, we were in the same class at USC, where he played baseball and later in the major leagues.

I talked to him about my frustration of not being able to move very we and how I could adjust to my physical limitations. He set me up with anoth pro, who taught me a strategy of how to play within those limitations.

For many years, I thought I'd never be able to compete in any sport again That has now changed, and I've found renewed joy in competing without stress and anxiety.

I'm a competitive athlete again.

The joy of competing without the drive to win at all costs, and yet, to always test myself to improve my skills — plus the game's comradery — that's why playing pickleball gives me so much joy.

I thank God for my competitive drive and for the athletic skills He's given me over my entire life.

Once again, at age 78, I feel like that adventuresome little boy in the backyard — *before* he got his fingers mangled by the lawn mower.

You know, the one with the high pain threshold who doesn't like to be told that he can't do something.

Except when God speaks, I listen and obey His Word.

For from Him and through Him and to Him are all things.
To Him be the glory forever.
Amen.
ROMANS 11:36

Made in the USA
Las Vegas, NV
20 April 2023

70862975R00195